Luca Moretti

AIR FRYER Cookbook

200 Quick & Easy

Recipes For Healthy Oil Free Living

P

PerseuS press

PerseuS
press

Contents

Introducing the Air Fryer   **1**

The Air Fryer at Work   **5**

Choosing the Right Air Fryer for your Needs 6

Features of your New Air Fryer...7

The Benefits of Using an Air Fryer..8

Getting the Most Out of your Air Fryer 9

Breakfast   **11**

Granola Bars 13

Chocolate Pancakes 14

Cinnamon Banana Muffins 15

Whole Grain Raspberry Muffins 16

Oats and Chia Porridge 17

Cheese and Bacon Wraps..18

Mushroom Baked Ham 19

Strawberry Vanilla Pancake..20

Broccoli and Potatoes Scramble 21

Bacon and Eggs Sandwich 22

Baked Polenta Bites 23

Carrot and Raisin bars...24

Bagels 25

Cinnamon Butter Toast 26

Chicken Burritos 27

Full English Breakfast 28

Roasted Baby Potatoes 29

Frittata 30

Baked Spinach and Ham Eggs 31

Cheese and Mushroom Frittata 32

Banana Flapjacks 33

Creamy and Cheesy Pancake 34

Vegetarian Omelet 35

Bacon and Cheese Rolls 36

Meatballs and Creamy Potatoes 37

Sweet Potato Fritters 38

Berries Pancakes 39

PB & Mallow Turnovers 40

Meat   41

Meatballs and Spaghetti 43

Asian Peppered Beef Ribs 44

Pesto Sirloin Steak 45

Beef Kofta 46

Beef Liver Curry 47

Lamb Flat Breads 48

Singapore Beef Noodles 49

Lamb Saltimbocca 50

Zesty Meatballs 51

Spinach and Blue Cheese Meat Loaf 52

Ham Risotto 53

Chinese Kebabs 54

Apple Curry Beef...55

Orange Pecan Crusted Lamb...56

Beef Stuffed Acorn Squash 57

Roasted Leg of Lamb with Pumpkin..58

Air Fryer Beef Stuffed Bell Peppers...59

Air-Fried Beef Burgers...60

Stuffed Zucchini with Bacon and Jalapeno...61

Mushroom Topped Pork Chops..62

Baby Back Ribs 63

Sausage Fettuccine...64

Pineapple Ribs...65

Ham and Onion Biscuits..66

Beef and Broccoli 67

Air Fried Meatloaf..68

Rib Eye-Steak..69

Zucchini Bacon Cheesy Lasagna..70

Poultry 71

Cheesy Chicken Spaghetti..73

Chicken and Tomato Rice...74

Air Fried Turkey Breast..75

Chicken and Gravy Over Noodles..76

Chicken and Tomato Risotto...77

Chicken n' Biscuits..78

Chicken and Cabbage Spring Rolls 79

Basil and Garlic Chicken Legs...80

Chicken Veggie Bake...81

Marjoram Chicken Breasts..82

Sweet and Lemony Stuffed Chicken 83

Garlic and Lime Chicken Breasts...84

Air Fried Cordon Bleu 85

Maple Glazed Turkey Breast 86

Jamaican Chicken Meatballs 87

Air-Fried Ravioli 88

Air Fried Mac 'n Cheese 89

Chicken on Olives and Prunes 90

Turkey Tortilla Rolls 91

Fresh Rosemary Chicken 92

Chicken Thighs with Rice and Broccoli 93

Chicken Kebabs 94

Indian-Style Chicken 95

Asian Air Fried Chicken 96

Sherry and Marsala Chicken 97

Chicken on Skewers 98

Chicken Nuggets 99

Pineapple BBQ Chicken Kebabs 100

Seafood   101

Seafood Spaghetti 103

Coconut Fried Shrimp 104

Salmon Risotto 105

Shrimp and Mushroom Risotto 106

Salmon Quiche 107

Air Fried Catfish 108

Cedar Plank Salmon 109

Halibut Sitka 110

Air Fried Calamari and Tomato Pasta 111

Air Fried Chili Octopus 112

Air Fried Dragon Shrimp 113

Chinese Mushroom Tilapia 114

Air Fried Spinach Fish 115

Fish Lettuce Wraps 116

Tuna Risotto 117

Air Fried Perch 118

Shrimp Spaghetti 119

Prawn Curry 120

Asian Tilapia 121

Tandori Fish 122

Pecan Crusted Salmon 123

Crusted Halibut 124

Cheesy Bacon Wrapped Shrimp 125

Crab Cakes 126

Tuna with Fusilli Pasta 127

Chinese Fried White Fish 128

Salmon and Dill Bites 129

Cayenne Tuna Puffs 130

Sides   131

French Bread 133

Onion Beer Bread 134

Roasted Vegetable Rice 135

Coconut Bread 136

Cheesy Spaghetti 137

Spinach Stuffed Cannelloni 138

Classic Dinner Rolls 139

Cheesy Stuffed Manicotti 140

Saffron Risotto 141

Air Fried Cinnamon Biscuits 142

Asparagus and Parmesan Risotto 143

Butternut Squash Risotto 144

Egg, Ham, and Cheese Biscuits 145

Mayo Broccoli and Cauliflower Egg Salad with Bacon................................146

Roasted Pear and Roquefort Salad with Pecans 147

Cranberry and Blue Cheese Roasted Carrot Salad 148

Cranberry, Almond, and Poppy Seed Cabbage Salad 149

Paprika Potato Wedges 150

Cheesy Potato Gratin 151

Spicy Couscous with Peas and Chickpeas 152

Sherry Green Beans 153

Baked Potatoes with Pepper and Onion..154

French Fries...155

Breaded Onion Rings 156

Baked Potatoes 157

Roasted Mushrooms..158

Mashed Potato Cakes 159

Roasted Brussels Sprouts 160

Air Fried Veggie Manchurian..161

Air Fried Samousa 162

Veggie and Cashew Rolls...163

Vegetarian Bean Patties...164

Snacks & Appetizers   165

Garlicky Zucchini Fries...167

Chips with Creamy and Cheesy Dip 168

Lemony Roasted Bell Peppers..169

Garlicky Eggplant Chips 170

Crunchy Onion Rings..171

Cheesy Slider..172

Onion-Cheese Puff Bites 173

Ham-Broccoli Quiche 174

Mexican Empanada 175

Homemade Sunflower Bread 176

Mushroom-Salami Pizza 177

Breaded Calamari with Salsa Dip 178

Thai-Inspired Vegan Spring Rolls 179

Fish Croquettes 180

Mushroom Roast 181

Poked Potatoes 182

Crispy Potato Wedges with Paprika 183

Classic French Fries 184

Meatballs with Mexican Sauce 185

Fried Shrimps in Bacon Blanket 186

Cheesy Croquettes 187

Feta Bites 188

Korean Style Chicken BBQ 189

Meatballs with Yogurt Dip 190

Air Fried Pigs in a Blanket 191

Stuffed Portobello 192

Mini Calzone 193

Air Fried Corn Dogs 194

Desserts   195

Chocolate Brandy Cake 197

Chocolate Cherry Tart 198

Apple Pie 199

Air Fried Chocolate Cake 200

Chocolate Caramel Peanut Cake 201

Cinnamon Doughnuts 202

Chocolate Orange Fudge Cake..203

Peanut Butter Chocolate Poke Cake 204

Chocolate Peanut Butter Cake..205

Triple Chocolate Cheese cake 206

Air Fried Banana Cake 207

Chocolate Chiffon Cake 208

Scones 209

Chocolate Espresso Cake..210

Dark Chocolate Truffles 211

Strawberry Butter Cake 212

Rum Cake...213

Date Nut Loaf..214

Carrot Raisin Bread..215

Chocolate Zucchini Bread..216

Chocolate Biscuits..217

Banana Walnut Bread...218

Palmier Biscuits..219

Chocolate Volcano Cake 220

Gran's Apple Cake 221

Cherry Almond Cake..222

Lemon Berry Cake 223

Lazy Dump Cake 224

Conclusion   **225**

Introducing the Air Fryer

Almost all Americans love that *crunchy texture* and intense flavor of delicious deep fried foods like fried chicken, French fries, battered pork chops and crispy calamari.

No wonder these dishes are staples, not only in fast food restaurants but also in households menus of many across the US, if not worldwide.

While this may be true, everyone is also seeking to be fit, radiant and healthy. The unfortunate truth us that the words "*healthy & fried*" do not harmonize in our current western lexicon and most health experts and fitness guru's tell us to avoid these tasty fried dishes altogether.

According to doctors and experts, the Standard American diet is extremely high in fat and very low in micronutrients due to *the low quality, non-organic ingredients* used in American kitchens nowadays.

Current scientific research has shown time and time again that the average Western dietary pattern consisting of **unhealthy oils, fats and high-glycemic carbohydrates** are undeniably linked to obesity and various chronic diseases of lifestyle. Recent studies performed at the ***John Hopkins University of Medicine*** confirms that regular consumption of fried foods increases the risk of heart disease and type 2 diabetes tenfold.

A scary thought considering that **48%** of all deaths are caused by heart disease and **1.5 million** die of a diabetic related illness.

Deep frying, which is one of the most popular cooking methods in the United States and many Western countries, is pointed out to be the main reason to blame.

Okay, I know what you are thinking – *"enough with the morbid talk already, we've heard it a million times before!"*

So does this mean that we can no longer enjoy our deep-fried favorites? Fortunately, the answer is a confounding….. NO.

By purchasing this book, I know that you probably have an idea of how powerful this device can be in transforming a so called ***"unhealthy, oily meal"*** into one that even a strict health fanatic will approve of.

The air fryer was designed specifically for this purpose—so that people can enjoy fried foods without the health drawbacks.

After all, why can't you have your cake and eat it? Or in this case, fry you French fries and devour **ALL** of them?

This revolutionary new appliance has gained quite the following has found its way to print, internet and broadcast media as well as into some of the most well know celebrities kitchens – Kim Kardashian to name one of them.

But, how does it work you ask? By using extremely high heat from convection currents to heat the air around the food without the use of excessive oil.

It first hit the scene in Europe and Australia around 2010 and was eventually introduced in North America around 2011.

In Japan and various other Asian countries, it's now being used to create crunchy tempura dishes. In London, it's what people use for whipping their all too familiar fish and chips.

And in the United States, the air fryer is slowly becoming the go-to device for frying burgers, meatballs, chicken and our favorite….French fries.

But it doesn't end there, with an air fryer you end up with healthier, low-fat dishes that make use of little to no oil. As for the flavor and texture, we'll let you be the judge after try a few recipes in this book.

Most lay people report they can't taste any difference between deep-fried foods and air-fried foods. To top this off the Air Fryer is one of *the easiest* devices to use and clean up.

This book will spotlight whether it really deserves the attention it is currently getting in the culinary space, and if it is all it is made out to be.

When it's a complete guide on how to use this amazing kitchen appliance and maximize its benefits you truly realize all the amazing benefits that you can enjoy with this technologically advanced kitchen appliance, you will easily get excited about the delicious yet healthy food that you are now able to serve your family in just a few easy steps.

We've put together a plethora of unique and diverse recipes that you can try and tweak to your taste and preferences, and best of all they won't take too much time or effort to make.

Wait no longer –the journey to simple, delicious and health Air Fried meals starts now!

The Air Fryer at Work

Before you get started with your air fryer and learning the benefits, it helps to know exactly how this cooking appliance works.

Now most of us might be thinking that air fryers are limited to cooking only, but in reality it is a multipurpose device as it can fry, roast, grill, and bake delicious, mouth-watery meals.

An air fryer utilizes a method called *"Rapid Air Technology"* to cook food that usually requires being submerged in a deep basket of fat or oil.

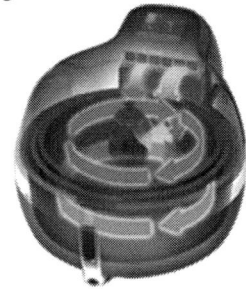

The device rapidly circulates heated air causing it to reach over 350 degrees F at times, and this it effortlessly fries foods like fries, chicken, chips, fish and much more.

The cooking chamber gives off enough heat to cook it thoroughly and it houses an exhaust fan that promotes air flow so that the heated air constantly passes through the chosen food that you've placed inside.

To put it simply, all parts of the food are heated at the same temperature at the same time.

Primarily designed to use up to **80 percent less** fat than the traditional deep fryer, a serving of potato fries which usually requires up to one cup of cooking oil, will only need a tbsp. of oil in the air fryer.

Not only that but the air fryer will cook the same meal in less than half the time.

Choosing the Right Air Fryer for your Needs

Here is a list of some air fryer brands in the market. Find out which one is the best for you:

Phillips XL Air fryer: A large capacity device, making it a perfect choice for families or anyone who wishes to fry large batches at once. This air fryer brand is also good for roasting, baking, and steaming ingredients. It comes with a dishwasher-safe for a smooth clean-up, a touch-screen interface, an adjustable temperature up to around 390 degrees, and a 60-minute timer.

GoWISE USA GW22621 Electric Air Fryer: This brand has an adjustable temperature range of 175 to 390 degrees and can cook meals under 30 minutes. This air fryer is a practical choice for smaller families or for anyone who doesn't cook large batches frequently. The touch screen is simple and has seven inbuilt programs. You can pick from the general food items including chips, chicken, fish, fries, and meat.

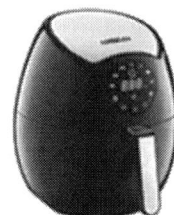

Power Air Fryer XL: This air fryer uses cyclonic heated air which cooks foods precisely and evenly for a delicious savory result without using any added oil. Other than that it comprises of an automated touch screen, and seven presets for popular meal items including chicken, fries, steaks, and baking goods.

Avalon Bay Digital Air Fryer: This brand comes with a fan that removes excess fats and oils from the food before air frying. The circulated air is then moved at a high speed to cook and heat the food efficiently for an even result. Also, this air fryer is perfect for baking, roasting, and grilling food items. The temperature for this brand ranges from 200 to 400 degrees and some customers claim you can use wet-battered ingredients with no expected splattering effects. It also has a non-slip rubber pad to hold the air fryer firmly in place.

NuWave Brio Air Fryer: This air fryer is good for cooking foods faster and simpler. This brand comes with of a preheat function, which brings the fryer to the best possible cooking temperature for your foods. It also has a digital touch screen to adjust the temperature and time. Also in this brand to ensure safety, the air frying process won't begin until the fry bucket is fully locked.

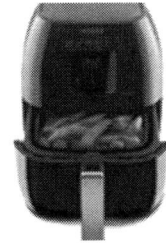

Features of your New Air Fryer

Highly Portable

Designed to easily be transferred from your kitchen storage cabinet to the countertop or to and from any place in your home – making it great to take to a friend for a cook off!

Automatic Temperature control

Get a perfectly cooked food every time. Just set your air fryer to your desired temperature and you can be assured that it will effortlessly cook your food to the desired doneness.

Digital touch Screen

No need to have to learn about complicated cooking maneuvers or have master culinary skills to use your air fryer. Simplicity is inbuilt with this feature. Most models allow you to set your cooking preferences with just a few taps on the touch panel's screen and voila, you are good to go.

Timer and buzzer

No need to worry about having to constantly keep an eye on your food or about accidentally overcooking it. With this feature you are frequently given audio cues on the progress of your meal.

Cooking Presets

This is the *silver bullet* of air fryers repertoire as it completely eliminates the need to set cooking times and temperatures for your commonly cooked foods. Ingredient specifications are preprogrammed into the appliance an all you have to do is choose the correct one, and with the push of a button the preset has got you covered.

The Benefits of Using an Air Fryer

First and foremost, the air fryer became popular for its numerous health benefits. The convenience and ease of use area close second and this combination makes it and easy choice for those who want a healthy, delicious meal in a fraction of the time. For those who doubt the air fryer capabilities and prefer conventional cooking methods, perhaps the following points will be enough to convince them to make the switch to efficient cooking:

Massive reduction in oil –no more than a tsp or two of f oil is needed to cook food in an air fryer and yet it still achieves the same texture. A far cry from the many cups of oil that you would have to use to cook food in a deep fryer. The result is food that is not soaked in unhealthy fat that will clogg the arteries.

Bursting with flavor – the flavor of the food truly comes out in an air fryer. Despite the small amount of oil used in "frying" the food, the "fried" taste and texture is achieved.

Easy press-and-go operation –No longer do you need to watch over your frying pan on your stove while frying your food. This also means no splattering of oil and accidental burns. All of the magic happens in the cooking chamber, just set your cooking preferences, push the right button, and let the air fryer do all of the work.

Rapid cooking times –The high temperatures that are circulated in the cooking chamber cut common cooking times in half. This is because the heat is maintained throughout the time being cooked meaning you do not have to worry about loss of heat slowing down you cooking.

Cleaning made Easy –With food baskets that are dishwasher safe it's as simple as removing it and putting it in. The cooking chamber can easily be cleaned with a cloth and a mild dishwashing soap.

Versatile unmatched – this modern appliance is more than just a fryer. You can bake, grill, and broil in it too. More of a highly versatile, mini convection oven rather than a fryer.

Safe – Its components are food safe and the cooking process itself helps you avoid kitchen accidents that can result in oil burns. The body of the air fryer hardly gets hot even if the temperature inside is at its highest. Using your standard kitchen gloves will give you more than enough protection when handling this kitchen appliance.

These benefits make air fryers the obvious choice when it comes to healthy cooking No compromise on flavor or convenience!

Getting the Most Out of your Air Fryer

To maximize the benefits of using an air fryer, here are some tips that you should not overlook:

Getting Started

▶ Place your air fryer on a level and heatproof kitchen top, if you have granite surfaces this is perfect.
▶ Avoid putting it close to the wall as this will dissipate the heat causing slower cooking times. Leave a space of at least five inches between the wall and the air fryer.
▶ Oven-safe baking sheets and cake pans may be used in the air fryer on the condition that they can fit inside easily and the door can close.

Before Cooking

▶ If you can, always preheat your air fryer for 3 minutes before cooking. Once the timer goes off it will be ready to rock and roll.
▶ Use a hand pumped spray bottle for applying the oil. Adopting this method will cause you to use less oil and is an easier option when compared to brushing or drizzling. Avoid caned aerosol brands as they tend to have a lot of nasty chemicals

▶ Always Bread if necessary. This breading step should not be missed. Be sure to press the breading firmly onto the meat or vegetable so the crumbs do not fall off easily.

Whilst Cooking

▶ Adding water into the air fryer drawer while cooking high fat foods to will prevent excessive smoke and heat. Use this technique when cooking burgers, bacon, sausage and similar foods.

▶ Secure light foods such as bread slices with toothpicks so they don't get blown around.

▶ Avoid putting too many food items into the air fryer basket. Overcrowding will result in uneven cooking and will also prevent the food from getting that glorious crispy texture that we all love.

▶ Shaking the fryer and flipping the food halfway through the cooking process is advised to make sure that everything inside cooks evenly.

▶ Opening the air fryer a few times to check how the food is doing won't affect the cooking time, so don't worry.

Once done:

▶ Remove the basket from the drawer before taking out the food to prevent the oil remaining one the food that you just fried.

▶ The juices in the air fryer drawer can be used to make delicious marinades and sauces. If you find it too greasy you can always reduce it in a saucepan to get rid of the excess liquid.

▶ Cleaning both the basket and drawer after every use is imperative.

Now that you've gotten to know the basics of using the air fryer, let's get to the exciting part—it's cooking time!

Breakfast

Granola Bars

(Total Time: 40 MIN | Serves: 12)

Ingredients:

1 cup butter, melted

2 cups dry oats

1 cup sunflower seeds

½ walnuts, chopped

¼ cup honey

¼ cup peanut butter

1 tsp. ground cinnamon

1 cup dried cranberries, chopped

Directions:

1. Preheat the air fryer to 325 degrees F. Spray a baking pan with nonstick spray.

2. Place the oats, seeds, and walnuts on a baking tray and bake in the air fryer for 10 minutes. Remove and let cool.

3. Once cool, mix all ingredients together and press into a baking pan. Bake for 30 minutes.

4. Let cool and slice into bars.

5. Enjoy!

Chocolate Pancakes

(Total Time: 35 MIN | Serves: 10)

Ingredients:

1 cup milk

1 egg

2 tbsp. butter, melted

1 cup butter

½ cup cocoa powder

¼ cup sugar

1 tsp baking soda

½ tsp. salt

½ cup fresh raspberries

Directions:

1. Preheat air fryer to 320 degrees F.
2. In a large bowl, combine the milk, egg, and butter. Whisk until smooth.
3. In a second bowl, combine remaining ingredients, except for raspberries. Mix well.
4. Gradually add the egg mixture to the flour mixture. Mix just until combined.
5. Carefully pour ¼ cup of the mixture onto the fryer tray. Cook for 2 to 3 minutes. Repeat with remaining batter.
6. Top with fresh raspberries and enjoy!

Cinnamon Banana Muffins

(Total Time: 18 MIN | Serves: 4)

Ingredients:

¼ cup Oats

4 tbsp. All-Purpose Flour

¼ cup mashed Banana

1 tbsp. chopped Walnuts

½ tsp Cinnamon

1 tbsp. Milk

¼ cup Powdered Sugar

¼ cup Butter

½ tbsp. Baking Powder

Pinch of Salt

Directions:

1. Preheat your Air Fryer to 300 degrees F.
2. In a bowl, combine the oats, flour, cinnamon, salt, and baking powder.
3. In a mixing bowl, beat together the butter and sugar until creamy.
4. Beat in the mashed banana.
5. Combine the two mixtures together and stir in the milk and walnuts.
6. Line or grease 4 muffin cups.
7. Divide the batter between them.
8. Place the muffin cups in your Air Fryer.
9. Bake for 10 minutes.
10. Serve and enjoy!

Whole Grain Raspberry Muffins

(Total Time: 16 MIN | Serves: 6)

Ingredients:

3 eggs

1 cup Cream Cheese

1 cup Coconut Milk

1 cup Coconut Sugar (or Brown Sugar)

¼ tsp Vanilla Powder (or 1 tsp Vanilla Extract)

2 tbsp. Maple Syrup

1 cup Whole Grain Flour

½ cup Ground Flaxseed

1 tsp Baking Powder

1 pinch Salt

1 cup Raspberries

Directions:

1. Place eggs in a mixing bowl and whisk well.
2. Add the cream cheese, coconut milk and sugar, vanilla powder and maple syrup, and whisk to combine, about 2 minutes.
3. Preheat the Air fryer to 390 degrees F.
4. Add the whole grain flour, flaxseed, baking powder and salt, and stir well until the batter is smooth, about 2 minutes.
5. Add raspberries and gently stir to combine.
6. Fill muffin cups two-thirds full with this batter and bake in your Air fryer for 10 minutes.
7. Serve with a hot cocoa.
8. Enjoy!

Oats and Chia Porridge

(Total Time: 8 MIN | Serves: 4)

Ingredients:

1 tbsp. Almond Butter

4 cups Coconut Milk

1 tbsp. Coconut Oil

4 tbsp. Maple Syrup

1 cup Chia Seeds

1 cups Steel Cut Oats

Directions:

1. Set your Air fryer to 390 degrees F to preheat for 3 minutes.
2. While the Air fryer is preheating place the almond butter, coconut milk and oil, and maple syrup in a bowl and whisk well to combine, around 1 minute.
3. Add chia seeds and oats and stir to combine.
4. Transfer in a baking accessory and place in the Air fryer for five minutes, to just warm up.
5. Stir well before serving garnished with fresh seasonal berries of your choice.

Cheese and Bacon Wraps

(Total Time: 20 MIN | Serves: 3)

Ingredients:

3 tbsp. Cream Cheese

2 Scrambled Eggs

3 Corn Tortillas

6 Fried Rashers of Bacon

3 tbsp. Mild Salsa

1 cup Pepper Jack Cheese

Directions:

1. Place the salsa and cream cheese in a bowl, mix together and set aside.
2. Warm up tortillas, either by placing in a microwave oven for 2-3 30 seconds bursts, or in a dry skillet over medium high heat for 30 seconds on each side.
3. Set the Air fryer to 390 degrees F to preheat.
4. Divide the salsa and cream cheese in thirds and spread on each of tortillas.
5. Roughly crumble the scrambled eggs and place a third on each of the tortillas.
6. On one half, a bit off center, of each tortilla place two fried bacon rashers.
7. Grate cheese on top of the bacon.
8. Fold over the half with stuffing so that edge reaches the middle of tortilla, then fold over the adjoining sides so that edge reaches quarter or so of the diameter of tortilla, then fold over and tuck under the free side to roll up the wraps.
9. Place in the Air fryer for 10 minutes.

Mushroom Baked Ham

(Total Time: 7-10 MIN | Serves: 1)

Ingredients:

1 Knob of Butter

8 Small Button Mushrooms

8 Cherry Tomatoes

6 slices Honey Shaved Ham

½ cup Cheddar Cheese

½ tbsp. Rosemary

½ tsp Chopped Garlic (or ¼ tsp Garlic Powder)

1 tbsp. Olive oil

Salt to taste

Ground Black Pepper to taste

2 eggs

2 Whole Wheat Croissants

Directions:

1. Quarter the mushrooms, halve the tomatoes and roughly chop the ham slices, and place them together in a bowl.
2. Preheat the Air fryer to 390 degrees F.
3. Add shredded cheddar cheese, finely chopped rosemary, garlic, olive oil and salt and pepper to taste, and gently mix everything to coat with olive oil.
4. Grease a baking accessory with the butter and place the mixture in it.
5. Push away the mixture to make two wells and crack an egg in each of them, and season the eggs with salt and pepper to taste.
6. Bake for 5 to 8 minutes depending on desired doneness of eggs.
7. Serve on the sliced open croissants with a side of salad greens. Optionally you can place croissants sliced open in the Air fryer during the last minute of baking to warm them up.

Strawberry Vanilla Pancake

⏱ 🍽
(Total Time: 20 MIN | Serves: 4)

Ingredients:

3 Eggs

1 pinch Salt

1 cup Coconut Milk

3 ½ Butter, melted and at room temperature

¼ tsp Vanilla Powder (or 1 tsp Vanilla Extract)

2 tbsp. Maple Syrup

1 cup Coconut Sugar (or Brown Sugar)

1 cup Rice Flour

1 cup Whole Grain Flour

2 tsp Baking Powder

½ cup Strawberries

2-3 tbsp. Batter or Coconut oil

Directions:

1. Place the eggs and pinch of salt in a bowl and whisk well.
2. Add coconut milk, melted butter, vanilla powder, coconut sugar and maple syrup in the bowl and whisk well till the sugar is melted, 1-2 minutes.
3. Preheat your Air fryer to 390 degrees F with a baking accessory in it.
4. Sift in the bowl rice and whole grain flour and baking powder.
5. Mix the batter as any pancake batter, until there are no lumps bigger than ⅛ of an inch.
6. Add the strawberries and stir gently to combine.
7. Grease the bottom of baking accessory with small amount of butter or coconut oil.
8. Ladle the butter and bake for 5 minutes.
9. Repeat until all of the batter is used.
10. Serve with honey or maple syrup.

Broccoli and Potatoes Scramble

(Total Time: 28 MIN | Serves: 4)

Ingredients:

1 Tofu Block, cut to 1 inch cubes

½ cup Onion, finely chopped

2 tbsp. Soy Sauce

1 tsp Ground Turmeric

½ tsp Onion powder

½ tsp Garlic powder

2 tbsp. Olive Oil

2 ½ cup Red Potatoes, cut to 1 inch cubes

4 cups Broccoli florets

Salt to taste

Ground Black Pepper to taste

Directions:

1. Preheat the Air fryer to 400 degrees F.
2. Place in a bowl the soy sauce, one tbsp. of olive oil, turmeric, onion and garlic powder, salt and pepper to taste, and whisk to combine.
3. Add the tofu and chopped onions. Toss to coat and set aside.
4. In another bowl place the potatoes, one tbsp. of olive oil and salt and pepper to taste, and toast as well to coat.
5. Place potatoes in the Air fryer basket and bake for 10 minutes. Shake once or twice during the baking.
6. Add the marinated tofu, including the marinade, toss to mix well. Bake for another 10 minutes shaking once or twice during baking.
7. Add the broccoli and toss to mix. Bake for another 6 minutes.
8. Enjoy!

Bacon and Eggs Sandwich

(Total Time: 11 MIN | Serves: 1)

Ingredients:

1 Egg

2 rashers of Bacon

1 English muffin, sliced open

Salt to taste

Ground Black Pepper to taste

Directions:

1. Preheat the Air Fryer at 400 degrees F for 3 minutes.
2. Cut bacon slices in half and set aside.
3. Crack the egg into a ramekin and sprinkle with salt and pepper.
4. Place the ramekin in the Air Fryer, and muffin halves with the crust side down next to.
5. Place two halves of bacon rashers on each muffin half.
6. Bake for 6 minutes.
7. To assemble the sandwich place the bottom half of muffin with bacon on a plate, then place the egg on it. Next place the top half of muffin with bacon and slice the whole sandwich in half.
8. Enjoy!

Baked Polenta Bites

⏱ 🍽

(Total Time: 60 MIN | Serves: 1)

Ingredients:

3 cups Water

3 tbsp. Butter

A pinch of Salt

1 cup Yellow Cornmeal

2 tbsp. Coconut Oil

Maple Syrup for serving

Directions:

1. Pour water in a saucepan and bring to boil over high heat.
2. Add the butter to water and lower the heat to medium.
3. Slowly add cornmeal to water while stirring constantly.
4. Cook until it thickens to mashed potatoes consistency while constantly stirring, some 12 minutes. To prevent splatters stir more and more vigorously as it thickens.
5. Remove from heat and leave to cool for 30 minutes.
6. Preheat the Air Fryer to 380 degrees F.
7. Form the polenta into balls the size of a golf balls.
8. Place balls in the Air Fryer basket and drizzle them with small amount of coconut oil.
9. Bake for 8 minutes, flip them over and cook another 8 minutes.
10. Serve warm and drizzled with maple syrup.
11. Enjoy!

Carrot and Raisin bars

(Total Time: 25 MIN | Serves: 2)

Ingredients:

¼ cup of honey

3 cups oats

1 cup almond butter

½ cup raisins

½ cup grated carrot

½ cup shredded sweetened
   coconut

¼ cup slivered almonds

Directions:

1. Preheat the air fryer to 350 degrees F. Spray a baking pan with non stick spray.
2. Combine all ingredients and mix very well. Press into the prepared baking pan.
3. Bake for 20 minutes.
4. Cool completely, slice into bars and serve.
5. Enjoy!

Bagels

(Total Time: 20 MIN | Serves: 12)

Ingredients:

½ lb. flour

1 tsp. active dry yeast

1 tsp. brown sugar

½ cup lukewarm water

2 tbsp. butter, softened

1 tsp salt

1 large egg

Directions:

1. Dissolve the yeast and sugar in the warm water. Let rest for 5 minutes.
2. Add the remaining ingredients and mix until a sticky dough forms. Cover and let rest for 40 minutes.
3. Knead the dough on a lightly floured surface and divide into 5 large balls. Let rest for 4 minutes.
4. Preheat air fryer to 360 degrees F.
5. Flatted the dough balls and make a hole in the center of each. Arrange the bagels on a baking sheet lined with parchment paper. Bake for 20 minutes.
6. Enjoy!

Cinnamon Butter Toast

(Total Time: 12-13 MIN | Serves: 6)

Ingredients:

½ cup Sugar

1 stick of Butter, at room temperature

A pinch of Ground Black Pepper

1 ½ tsp Cinnamon

1 ½ tsp Vanilla Extract

12 Whole Wheat Bread slices

Directions:

1. Place in a mixing bowl the butter, sugar, pepper, cinnamon and vanilla extract.
2. Mix with a fork until everything is fairly well combined and all sugar is incorporated into butter.
3. With a hand mixer mix the butter until almost all sugar has dissolved, around 2 minutes
4. Spread equally thick on all slices of bread.
5. Number of slices place on the bottom of Air Fryer basket and the rest on the metal holder or roasting rack if all slices cannot fit in a single layer.
6. Bake for 5 minutes at 400 degrees F.
7. Enjoy!

Chicken Burritos

(Total Time: 10-13 MIN | Serves: 2)

Ingredients:

2 Eggs

Salt to taste

Ground Black Pepper to taste

2 Corn Tortillas, 10 inch size

1 Chicken Breast, cooked and shredded

2 tbsp. Salsa

1 small Red Bell Pepper, diced

1 small Avocado, peeled and cubed

⅛ cup Mozzarella, shredded

Cooking spray

Directions:

1. Whisk eggs well and then salt and pepper them.
2. Pour the whisked eggs into Air Fryer accessory and cook for 5 minutes at 400 degrees F.
3. While eggs are cooking warm up tortillas by blitzing them for 30 seconds in a microwave.
4. Preheat the Air Fryer to 360 degrees F.
5. Shred the eggs with a fork and divide between tortillas, placing it on one half of tortilla a bit off center.
6. Add the shredded chicken, then salsa, bell pepper and avocado, and then the shredded mozzarella, all on top of the eggs.
7. Fold over the half with stuffing so that edge reaches the middle of tortilla, then fold over the adjoining sides so that edge reaches quarter or so of the diameter of tortilla, then roll up the burritos.
8. Place burritos in the Air Fryer basket and cook for 3 minutes.
9. Cut each burrito across at an angle and serve.
10. Enjoy!

Full English Breakfast

(Total Time: 30 MIN | Serves: 4)

Ingredients:

8 Bacon Rashers

8 Sausages

10 oz Canned Baked Beans, drained

8 Medium Eggs

16 Cherry Tomatoes, halved

16 Button Mushrooms, halved

Salt to taste

Ground Black Pepper to taste

8 Toast Slices

Directions:

1. Put sausages and bacon in the Air Fryer, use the grill pan accessory if available, and cook them for 10 minutes at 360 degrees F.
2. When done transfer them to serving plates.
3. While sausages and bacon are cooking take four 4 ounces ramekins and crack two eggs in each of them, add salt and pepper to taste.
4. Pour beans in a 10 ounces ramekin, add salt and pepper.
5. Place both ramekins with eggs and the one with beans in the Air Fryer and cook for 10 minutes at 400 degrees F.
6. Remove ramekins from the Air Fryer and place in it mushroom halves and cook them for 6 minutes at 400 degrees F.
7. Transfer eggs on the plates with bacon and sausages.
8. Stir beans and then spoon a quarter next to eggs on each plate.
9. Add the cherry tomatoes to the Air Fryer, sprinkle both mushrooms and tomatoes with salt and pepper to taste and cook for another 4 minutes at 400 degrees F.
10. Divide tomatoes and mushrooms to each plate.
11. Enjoy!

Roasted Baby Potatoes

(Total Time: 16 MIN | Serves: 4)

Ingredients:

1 ½ lbs Baby Potatoes, skinned and quartered

1 Red Bell Pepper, cut to 1 inch cubes

1 Medium Onion, diced

½ tsp Garlic Powder

1 tbsp. Olive oil

1 tsp Rosemary, chopped

Salt to taste

Ground Black Pepper to taste

Directions:

1. Preheat the Air Fryer to 400 degrees F.
2. Place all ingredients in a bowl and toss well to combine.
3. Cook in the Air Fryer for 15 minutes at 400 degrees, shaking twice during the cooking.
4. Enjoy!

30

Frittata

(Total Time: 15 MIN | Serves: 3)

Ingredients:

5 Baby Potatoes, cut to ½ inch cubes

1 tbsp. Olive Oil

1 Italian Sausage, cut to 1 inch slices

1 Red Bell Pepper, cut to 1 inch cubes

1 Small Onion, cut to 1 inch cubes

3 eggs

1 tbsp. Parsley Leaves, chopped

1 pinch Garlic Powder

2 tbsp. Grated Parmesan Cheese

Salt to taste

Ground Black Pepper to the taste

Directions:

1. Place baby potato cubes in the Air Fryer accessory, add the olive oil, salt and pepper to taste, and toss to mix well.
2. Cook for 5 minutes at 400 degrees F.
3. Add the sausage, bell pepper and onion to the Air Fryer accessory. Toss to mix and cook another 5 minutes at 400 degrees F.
4. Meanwhile whisk three eggs and then add to them the parsley, garlic powder, parmesan and pepper to taste, and stir well to combine.
5. Pour the egg mixture over potatoes and sausages in the Air Fryer accessory and cook for 10 minutes at 360 degrees F.
6. Serve warm.
7. Enjoy!

Baked Spinach and Ham Eggs

(Total Time: 25 MIN | Serves: 4)

Ingredients:

1 lbs Baby Spinach

1 tbsp. olive oil

1 tbsp. Butter, melted and cooled
to room temperature

7 oz Ham, grated

4 eggs

4 tbsp. milk

Salt and black pepper to the taste

Directions:

1. Warm up a pan over medium heat.
2. Add olive oil and spinach to pan. Toss and sauté for 2 minutes to wilt.
3. Brush four ramekins with melted butter.
4. Place a quarter of spinach in each of the ramekins, and add grated ham over it.
5. Also divide ham in each of the ramekins.
6. Crack an egg in each ramekin as well and top with the milk.
7. Season with salt and pepper, place ramekins in your air fryer's basket, cover and cook at 360 degrees F for 20 minutes.
8. Serve hot for breakfast.
9. Enjoy!

Cheese and Mushroom Frittata

(Total Time: 8-10 MIN | Serves: 4)

Ingredients:

4 cups Button Mushrooms, cut
   to ¼ inch slices

1 Large Red Onion, cut to ¼
   inch slices

2 tbsp. Olive Oil

1 tsp Garlic, minced

6 Eggs

Salt to taste

Ground Black Pepper to taste

6 tbsp. Feta Cheese

Directions:

1. Put the button mushrooms, onions and garlic in a pan with a tbsp. of olive oil, and sauté over medium heat for 5 minutes.
2. Transfer on a kitchen towel to dry and cool.
3. Preheat the Air Fryer to 330 degrees F.
4. Place eggs in a bowl and whisk lightly. Season with salt and pepper and then whisk well.
5. Brush the baking accessory with olive oil
6. Place sautéed onions and mushrooms in the baking accessory, crumble the feat cheese over it, and then pour the eggs on top.
7. Cook for 20 minutes or until a skewer stuck in the middle of frittata comes out clean.
8. Serve warm.
9. Enjoy!

Banana Flapjacks

(Total Time: 8-10 MIN | Serves: 2)

Ingredients:

1 Large Banana

2 Eggs

Olive Oil for greasing

Directions:

1. Preheat the Air Fryer to 330 degrees F.
2. Place in a bowl eggs and whisk them.
3. Add banana to eggs and lightly mash it with a fork.
4. Spoon quarters of mixture in the Air Fryer basket.
5. Cook for 3 minutes, then flip and cook for another 3 minutes.
6. Enjoy!

Ingredients:

2 Eggs

1 pack Stevia

½ tsp Cinnamon

2 cups Cream Cheese

Directions:

1. Preheat the Air Fryer to 330 degrees
2. Place the eggs and stevia in a bowl a whisk until stevia is dissolved.
3. Add the cinnamon and cream chees and whisk until smooth.
4. Ladle the quarter of batter into Air accessory and cook for 2 minutes at degrees F.
5. Flip the pancake and cook for 2 mo minutes.
6. Repeat for the rest of batter.
7. Enjoy!

Vegetarian Omelet

(Total Time: 16 MIN | Serves: 2)

Ingredients:

8 ounces spinach leaves

3 Spring Onions, cut to 1 inch slices

½ Red Bell Pepper, cut to 1 inch cubes

1 cup Button Mushrooms, cut to ¼ inch slices

½ tsp Ground Turmeric

1 tsp Thyme

1 tsp Kala Namak Salt

½ tsp Ground Black Pepper

1 tsp Minced Garlic

3 tbsp. Olive Oil (extra virgin)

2 tbsp. Butter

1 cup Chickpea Flour

1 cup Water

Directions:

1. In a bowl place spring onions, bell peppers, mushrooms, turmeric, thyme, kala namak salt, ground black pepper, minced garlic and two tbsp. of olive oil. Toss well to combine.
2. Heat a sauté pan over medium high heat and tip in the vegetables mixture.
3. Sauté for 3 minutes frequently tossing.
4. Add spinach and butter to the pan and sauté for another 3 minutes frequently tossing.
5. Remove from heat and set aside until needed.
6. In a bowl place the chickpea flour and water, and whisk to smooth batter.
7. Grease the Air Fryer accessory with olive oil and pour in the batter.
8. Cook for 3 minutes at 390 degrees F. Flip and cook for another 3 minutes.
9. Transfer fried omelet on a serving plate and top with sautéed vegetables.
10. Serve with salsa on the side.
11. Enjoy!

Bacon and Cheese Rolls

(Total Time: 8-10 MIN | Serves: 4)

Ingredients:

1 lbs Cheddar Cheese, grated

1 lbs Bacon Rashers

1 8 oz can Pillsbury Crescent Dough

Directions:

1. Preheat the Air Fryer to 330 degrees F.
2. Cut the bacon rashers across into ¼ inch strips and mix with the cheddar cheese. Set aside.
3. Cut the dough sheet to 1 by 1.5 inches pieces.
4. Place equal amount of bacon and cheese mixture on center of the dough pieces and pinch corners together to enclose stuffing.
5. Transfer the parcels in the Air Fry basket and bake for 7 minutes at 330 degrees F.
6. Increase the temperature to 390 degrees F, and bake for another 3 minutes.
7. Serve warm.
8. Enjoy!

Meatballs and Creamy Potatoes

(Total Time: 45-50 MIN | Serves: 4-6)

Ingredients:

12 oz Lean Ground Beef

1 Medium Onion, finely chopped

1 tbsp. Parsley Leaves, finely chopped

½ tbsp. Fresh Thyme Leaves

½ tsp Minced Garlic

2 tbsp. Olive Oil

1 tsp Salt

1 tsp Ground Black Pepper

1 Large Egg

3 tbsp. Bread Crumbs

1 cup Half & Half, or ½ cup Whole Milk and ½ cup Cream mixed together

7 Medium Russet Potatoes

½ tsp Ground Nutmeg

½ cup Grated Gruyere Cheese

Directions:

1. Place the ground beef, onions, parsley, thyme, garlic, olive oil, salt and pepper, egg and breadcrumbs in a bowl and mix well. Place in refrigerator until needed.
2. In another bowl place half & half and nutmeg, and whisk to combine.
3. Peel and wash potatoes, and then slice them thinly, ⅛ to ⊠ of an inch, if needed use a mandolin.
4. Preheat the Air Fryer to 390 degrees F.
5. Place potato slices in bowl with half & half and toss to coat well.
6. Layer the potato slices in an Air Fryer baking accessory and pour over the left over half & half.
7. Bake for 25 minutes at 390 degrees F.
8. Meanwhile take the meat mixture out of fridge and shape into inch and half balls.
9. When potatoes are cooked place meatballs on top of them in one layer and cover with the grated Gruyere.
10. Cook for another 10 minutes.
11. Enjoy!

Sweet Potato Fritters

(Total Time: 6-7 MIN | Serves: 4)

Ingredients:

1 can Sweet Potato Puree, 15 oz

½ tsp Minced Garlic

½ cup Frozen Spinach, thawed, finely chopped and drained well

1 Large Leek, minced

1 serving Flax Egg

¼ cup Almond Flour

¼ tsp Sweet Paprika Flakes

1 tsp Kosher Salt

½ tsp Ground White Pepper

Directions:

1. Preheat the Air Fryer to 330 degrees F.
2. Place all ingredients in a bowl and mix all well.
3. Divide in 16 balls and flatten each to no more than inch thick patty.
4. Place fritters in the Air Fryer basket and cook for two minutes at 330 degrees F.
5. Flip and cook for 2 more minutes.
6. If needed cook in batches.
7. Enjoy!

Berries Pancakes

(Total Time: 6-7 MIN | Serves: 1)

Ingredients:

1 cup Coconut Milk

2 tbsp. Coconut Oil

1 tsp Vanilla Extract

2 tbsp. Palm Sugar

1 pinch Kosher Salt

1 cup Whole Grain Flour

2 tsp Baking Powder

½ cup Blueberries

½ cup Cranberries

Honey or Maple Syrup for
drizzling

Directions:

1. Preheat the Air Fryer to 330 degrees F.
2. In a mixing bowl place coconut milk and oil, vanilla extract, palm sugar and salt. Whisk well to combine and palm sugar dissolves.
3. Sift in the mixing bowl flour and baking powder and stir to combine. Do not stir to smooth, but until there are no lumps larger than ⅛ of an inch.
4. Pour the butter in the Air Fryer accessory and cook for 2 minutes at 330 degrees F.
5. Flip the pancake and cook for another 2 minutes.
6. Transfer to a plate and drizzle with honey or maple syrup.
7. Enjoy!

PB & Mallow Turnovers

(Total Time: 25-30 MIN | Serves: 4)

Ingredients:

4 Filo Dough, defrosted

3 tbsp. Butter, melted and cooled to room temperature

4 tbsp. Peanut Butter, chunky kind and divided

4 tsp Marshmallow Fluff, divided

1 tbsp. Water

½ tsp Sea Salt

Directions:

1. Place one dough sheet on work surface and brush it with a tbsp. of butter. Place second dough sheet over the first one and brush it too. Repeat for the third sheet and then place fourth on top of it.
2. Cut the dough in four equal strips.
3. On one end of each strip score with a knife very shallow cut 3 inches from the narrower edge, for visual reference. Spread a tbsp. of peanut butter in marked square
4. If needed for visual reference, draw a diagonal line in peanut butter with tip of the knife.
5. Place a tsp of marshmallow fluff in center of the inside triangle of peanut butter.
6. Fold the corner without fluff over the one with, and continue folding in triangular shape.
7. When your reach the end of strip unroll the last fold and brush edges with small amount of water, and set it aside with the seal turned down.
8. Fold two more strips in the same fashion.
9. Preheat the Air Fryer to 360 degrees F while folding the fourth strip.
10. Place the triangles in Air Fryer basket, sprinkle with sea salt and bake for 10 minutes at 360 degrees F.
11. Let the turnovers rest for 10 minutes before serving.
12. Enjoy!

Meat

Meatballs and Spaghetti

(Total Time: 20 MIN | Serves: 4)

Ingredients:

1lbs. ground beef

½ cup panko bread crumbs

2 cloves garlic, minced

½ cup onion, minced

1 egg

2 tsp Italian seasoning

1lb dry spaghetti

½ cup grated parmesan

1 (24oz) marinara sauce

Directions:

1. Preheat fryer to 360 degrees F.
2. Combine the ground beef, panko, garlic, onion, egg, and Italian seasoning, mix well. Form into 2 inch balls.
3. Place in the fryer basked at cook for 20 minutes.
4. Meanwhile, bring a pot of water to a boil then add the pasta. Cook for 10 minutes or until tender. Drain and add the marinara sauce. Toss to coat the noodles
5. Remove meatballs and place on top of sauced spaghetti. Sprinkle Parmesan on top.
6. Serve and enjoy.

Asian Peppered Beef Ribs

(Total Time: 90 MIN | Serves: 4)

Ingredients:

2 racks bone in beef ribs, about 2
    pounds

2 tbsp. grated fresh ginger

2 cloves minced garlic

2 tsp. ground black pepper

1 tsp. salt

¼ cup dark brown sugar

2 tsp. Spanish paprika

2 tbsp. soy sauce

1 tbsp. Worcestershire sauce

Directions:

1. Combine all ingredients except for the ribs. Mix well to create a paste.

2. Coat each side of the beef ribs with ¾ of the seasoning paste. Reserve the remaining ¼ of the seasoning paste. Set aside and let rest for at least 15 minutes.

3. While the ribs rest, pre-heat the Air Fryer to 390 degrees F. Once hot, add the ribs cook for 1½ hours.

4. Once cooked, coat the ribs in remaining seasoning.

5. Enjoy!

Pesto Sirloin Steak

(Total Time: 25 MIN | Serves: 4)

Ingredients:

2 cups fresh basil leaves

3 cloves garlic

1 tsp salt

½ tsp. ground black pepper

2 tbsp. lemon juice

¼ cup olive oil

4 (8 ounce) sirloin steaks

Directions:

1. In a food processor, combine all ingredients except steak. Blend until well minced.
2. Spread half the mixture on to the steaks, reserve the remaining pesto. Let the steaks rest for 10 minutes.
3. Preheat flyer to 350 degrees F.
4. Once the 10 minutes rest period is up, place the steaks in the fryer basket and cook for 15 minutes.
5. Remove from the fryer and let rest for 5 minutes before slicing. Serve with remaining pesto on the side.
6. Enjoy!

Beef Kofta

🕐 **(Total Time: 25 MIN | Serves: 3)** 🍽️

Ingredients:

2 lbs. ground beef

½ cup yellow onion, diced small

¼ tsp. ground ginger

3 cloves garlic, minced

½ tsp ground turmeric

¼ cup fresh parsley, chopped

1 tsp. ground cumin

1 tbsp. tomato paste

½ tsp of Garam Masala

1 tsp ground coriander

½ tsp salt

¼ tsp ground black pepper

Directions:

1. Preheat the air fryer to 350 degrees F.
2. Combine all ingredients and mix well. Form the mixture in to mini loaves, about ¼ cup per loaf.
3. Spray the fryer try with nonstick spray and place the mini loaves on to the tray. Cooke for 20 minutes.
4. Remove and let sit for 5 minutes before serving.
5. Enjoy!

Beef Liver Curry

(Total Time: 20 MIN | Serves: 3)

Ingredients:

½ lb. beef liver, cut into 1 inch cubes

1 tsp. salt

½ tsp. ground black pepper

1 tbsp. olive oil

½ cup yellow onion, diced small

1 (14oz) can diced tomato

2 cloves garlic, minced

1 tbsp. tomato paste

1 tsp. ground ginger

½ tsp chili powder

1 tbsp. ground curry powder

1 tsp. ground cumin

½ tsp. ground coriander

½ tsp. turmeric

½ tsp. Garam Masala

½ tsp. honey

Directions:

1. Preheat fryer to 350 degrees.
2. Season the liver with salt and pepper. Place in the fryer basket and cook for 15 minutes.
3. Meanwhile, heat the olive oil in a large skillet. Once hot, add the onion and garlic. Cook just until the onions are soft then add the tomato paste, chili powder, cumin, curry, coriander, turmeric, and Garam Masala. Cook for one minute, stirring often.
4. Remove the liver from the fry and add to the skillet with the diced tomatoes and honey. Stir and simmer for 5 minutes.
5. Serve and enjoy!

Lamb Flat Breads

(Total Time: 30 MIN | Serves: 3)

Ingredients:

1 lb. ground lamb

2 tbsp. olive oil

1 red onion, thinly sliced

1 cup baby spinach

1 tsp. salt

½ tsp. ground black pepper

1 tsp. dried oregano

2 cloves garlic, minced

¼ cup toasted pine nuts

½ cup roasted red pepper, sliced thin

3 pre-made flat breads

1 cup crumbled feta

½ cup of fresh parsley leaves

Directions:

1. Preheat the air fryer to 390 degrees F.
2. Combine the lamb, salt, pepper, oregano, and garlic. Shape in to 1 inch balls and place in the fryer basket. Cook for 10 minutes.
3. Heat the remaining olive oil in a skillet. Once hot, add the onion, spinach, red pepper, and pine nuts. Cook until spinach is lightly wilted.
4. Remove the lamb from the air fryer. Top the flat breads with the spinach mixture and the lamb balls. Sprinkle with feta.
5. Bake the flat breads in the air fryer for 10 minutes. Remove and sprinkle with parsley.
6. Cut, serve, and enjoy!

Singapore Beef Noodles

(Total Time: 20 MIN | Serves: 4)

Ingredients:

1 lb. thinly sliced roast beef

1 tsp. salt

½ tsp ground black pepper

½ tsp. ground ginger

½ tsp. garlic powder

½ lb. cooked ramen noodles

3 tbsp. peanut oil

½ cup red onion, thinly sliced

½ cup shredded carrot

1 cup snow peas, thinly sliced

½ cup hoisin sauce

¾ cup roasted peanuts

½ cup fresh cilantro, chopped

Directions:

1. Preheat the air fryer to 390 degrees F.

2. Season the beef with the salt, pepper, ginger and garlic. Drizzle with 1 tbsp. of the oil and place in the air fryer and cook for 10 minutes.

3. Once the beef is cooked, heat the remaining oil in a skillet on high. Add the beef, onion, carrot, and snow peas. Cook until onion is soft. Stir in the hoisin, peanuts, and ramen.

4. Toss to combine ingredients and coat the noodles in the sauce. Simmer for 1 minute. Top with cilantro

5. Serve and enjoy!

Lamb Saltimbocca

(Total Time: 20 MIN | Serves: 5)

Ingredients:

12 thick cut lamb chop lollipops

1 lb. fresh mozzarella, cut into 1 inch cubes

8oz. thin sliced prosciutto, at least 12 pieces

12 whole sage leaves

2 tbsp. olive oil

1 tsp. salt

½ tsp. ground black pepper

Directions:

1. Preheat the air fryer to 350 degrees F.
2. Cut a pocket into the side of each lamb chop and stuff one cube of cheese inside of each pocket.
3. Season with salt and pepper and place 1 sage leaf on top of each lamb chop and then wrap each chop with a slice of prosciutto.
4. Place the wrapped lamb in the air fryer and drizzle with olive oil. Cook for 10 minutes.
5. Remove and let rest for 5 minutes before serving.
6. Enjoy!

Zesty Meatballs

(Total Time: 25 MIN | Serves: 3)

Ingredients:

1 lb. ground beef

½ cup yellow onion, diced

1 large egg

4 cloves garlic, minced

1 tsp. ground ginger

¼ red pepper flakes

½ cup Panko bread crumbs

Directions:

1. Preheat fryer to 360 degrees F.
2. Mix all ingredients well and form into 1 inch balls.
3. Place the balls on the fryer tray and cook for 15 minutes
4. Serve and Enjoy!

Spinach and Blue Cheese Meat Loaf

(Total Time: 40 MIN | Serves: 4)

Ingredients:

1½ lbs. ground beef

1 large egg

1 tsp Dijon mustard

½ cup ketchup

2 tsp. Worcestershire sauce

½ cup yellow onion, minced

1 tsp. salt

½ cup oats

½ tsp ground black pepper

1 cup cooked bacon, chopped

1 cup blue cheese crumbles

1 cup wilted spinach

Directions:

1. Preheat Air Fryer to 350 degrees F.
2. Combine all ingredients except for the bacon, spinach and blue cheese. Mix well.
3. Carefully add the bacon, spinach, and blue cheese. Mix gently and just until combined.
4. Spray the fryer tray with non-stick spray. Form the meat mixture into a loaf and place on the tray.
5. Cook for 90 minutes. Let rest for 10 minutes before slicing and serving.
6. Enjoy!

Ham Risotto

(Total Time: 35 MIN | Serves: 4)

Ingredients:

3 tbsp. olive oil

½ cup yellow onion, diced

1 cup ham, cut into small cubes

2 cups Arborio rice

½ cup dry white wine

4 cups chicken broth, warm

1 cup shredded cheddar cheese

Directions:

1. Preheat the air fryer to 320 degrees F.
2. Place the onion and ham in the fryer basket and drizzle with half the oil. Cook for 10 minutes.
3. Meanwhile, heat remaining oil in a large skillet. Add the rice and cook until lightly browned. Add the cooked ham and white wine.
4. Add 1 cup of the broth. Stir just until absorbed. Repeat with remaining broth.
5. Stir in cheddar cheese.
6. Serve and enjoy

Chinese Kebabs

(Total Time: 25 MIN | Serves: 2)

Ingredients:

1 lb. ground pork

½ cup yellow onion, diced small

2 cloves garlic, minced

1 tsp. grated fresh ginger

1 tbsp. of tomato puree

1 tbsp. Chinese five spice

1 cup Panko bread crumbs

1 tbsp. soy sauce

1 tsp. salt

½ tsp. ground black pepper

Directions:

1. Preheat air fryer to 390 degrees F.
2. Combine all ingredients in a large bowl and mix well.
3. Form the mixture into logs around skewers, about ¼ cup per log.
4. Place in frying tray and cook for 20 minutes.
5. Serve and enjoy!

Apple Curry Beef

(Total Time: 30 MIN | Serves: 4)

Ingredients:

1 apple, peeled, cored, and shredded

1 large yellow onion, chopped small

2 cloves garlic, minced

2 tbsp. curry

1 cup beef stock

1 ½ lbs. cubed stew beef

1 tbsp. olive oil

1 tsp. salt

½ tsp. ground black pepper

1/2 cup flour

2 tbsp. butter

Directions:

1. Preheat air fryer to 350 degrees F.
2. Combine half the flour, salt, and pepper. Toss the cubed beef in the flour mixture.
3. Place the beef into the fryer basket, drizzle with ½ the olive oil and cook for 20 minutes.
4. Meanwhile, heat the remaining olive oil in a soup pot. Once hot add the apple, onion, and garlic. Cook until onions are soft. Stir in the remaining flour and curry powder. Stir and cook for 2 minutes. Add the beef stock and whisk until smooth. Remove from heat.
5. Remove the beef from the fryer and add to the onion mixture. Bring to a simmer and simmer for 5 minutes. Remove from heat and stir in the butter.
6. Serve and enjoy!

Orange Pecan Crusted Lamb

(Total Time: 60 MIN | Serves: 4)

Ingredients:

2 racks lamb (about 2 and ½ lbs.)

½ tsp ground black pepper

1 tsp. salt

2 tbsp. olive oil

1 cup of fresh parsley leaves

2 cloves garlic, minced

2 tbsp. orange zest

2 tbsp. fresh rosemary

¾ cup pecans

2 tbsp. of Dijon mustard

Directions:

1. Preheat the air fryer to 390 degrees F. Season the lamb into the fryer and drizzle with half of the olive oil. Cook for 10 minutes.

2. Meanwhile, add remaining ingredients in a food processor and pulse just until crumbly and fine.

3. Remove the lamb from the fryer and coat with the spice mixture on all sides. Return to the fry and cook for 10 more minutes.

4. Serve and enjoy!

Beef Stuffed Acorn Squash

(Total Time: 20 MIN | Serves: 2)

Ingredients:

1 acorn squash, cut in half and
    seeds removed

1 tsp. salt

½ tsp. ground black pepper

½ lb. ground beef

¼ cup yellow onion, minced

2 cloves garlic, minced

½ tsp. ground cumin

½ tsp. paprika

½ tsp. dried basil

½ cup quinoa, cooked

Directions:

1. Preheat the air fryer to 390 degrees F. Place the acorn squash halves in the fryer basket and cook for 20 minutes.

2. While the squash cooks, heat a large skillet over medium heat. Add the ground beef and cook, breaking the meat in to small pieces, for 5 minutes. Stir in the remaining ingredients. Cook another 5 minutes or until beef is cooked through and onions are soft. Remove from heat.

3. Remove the squash from the air fryer. Spoon the beef mixture into the center of the squash.

4. Serve and enjoy.

Roasted Leg of Lamb with Pumpkin

(Total Time: 35 MIN | Serves: 4)

Ingredients:

1 ½ tsp. salt

1 tsp. ground black pepper

2 tsp lemon juice

1 tbsp. fresh rosemary, chopped

1 tbsp. fresh thyme, chopped

3 cloves garlic, minced

1 tbsp. grated parmesan cheese

2 tbsp. whole grain mustard

1 leg of lamb

2 tbsp. olive oil

1 medium pumpkin pie pumpkin, peeled, seeds removed, and cut into 1 inch chunks

Directions:

1. Preheat the air fryer to 390 degrees F. In a mixing bowl, combine salt, pepper, lemon juice, rosemary, thyme, garlic, and parmesan cheese.

2. Coat the lamb in the mustard and half of the seasoning mixture. Reserve the remaining seasoning for the pumpkin.

3. Place the lamb in the fryer basket, drizzle with olive oil, and cook for 20 minutes.

4. Toss the pumpkin chunks with the remaining seasoning mixture and the remaining olive oil.

5. Remove the lamb from the air fryer and let rest. Place the seasoned pumpkin into the fryer basket and cook for 15 minutes or until tender.

6. Slice the lamb and serve alongside the pumpkin, once cooked.

7. Serve and enjoy!

Air Fryer Beef Stuffed Bell Peppers

(Total Time: 35 MIN | Serves: 2)

Ingredients:

8-ounces of ground beef

2 bell peppers

2 minced garlic cloves

2-ounces of cheddar cheese, shredded

1 tsp of salt

2-ounces of mozzarella cheese, shredded

1 tsp of melted coconut oil

½ cup of tomato sauce

1 tsp of paprika

1 cup of chopped red onion

1 tsp of Worcestershire sauce

1 tsp of black pepper

Directions:

1. Cut the stem and deseed the bell peppers and boiled them for 3 minutes.
2. Preheat the air fryer to 390 degrees Fahrenheit. In a cooking pan add the coconut oil and wait until it melts.
3. Add the garlic, onion, and cook for a minute.
4. Transfer the onion mix to a bowl and add the beef.
5. Add the salt, black pepper, paprika, tomato sauce and waterside sauce.
6. Stuff the bell peppers using the beef mixture.
7. Add the cheese and tomato sauce on top.
8. Add the bell peppers into the air fryer and cook for about 20 minutes. Serve hot.

Air-Fried Beef Burgers

🕒
🍽️

(Total Time: 15 MIN | Serves: 4)

Ingredients:

1 pound of lean ground beef

1 tsp of black pepper

1 tbsp. of Worcestershire sauce

1 tsp of garlic powder

1 tsp of onion powder

1 tbsp. of dried parsley

1 tsp of salt

Directions:

1. Preheat the air fryer to 390 degrees Fahrenheit.
2. Combine the ground beef, salt, garlic powder, onion powder, parsley and Worcestershire sauce into a large mixing bowl.
3. Mix well and create burger patties using hands.
4. Fry the patties golden brown in the preheated air fryer.
5. Serve hot with buns.

Stuffed Zucchini with Bacon and Jalapeno

(Total Time: 15 MIN | Serves: 2)

Ingredients:

1 chopped jalapeno

3 zucchinis

1 cup of mozzarella cheese, shredded

1 tsp of black pepper

6 cooked and crumbled bacon slices

1 tbsp. of freshly chopped parsley

2 chopped tomatoes

1 (8-ounce) can of tomato sauce

1 tsp of salt

Directions:

1. Cut one end of the zucchinis and scoop out the seeds and flesh.
2. Combine the jalapeno, cheese, pepper, bacon, salt and parsley in a bowl.
3. Add the tomato sauce and mix well.
4. Use the mixture to fill in the zucchini.
5. Add to the air fryer and cook for about 10 minutes.
6. Serve hot.

Mushroom Topped Pork Chops

(Total Time: 40 MIN | Serves: 4)

Ingredients:

4 thick cut boneless pork chops

2 tbsp. olive oil

1 tsp. salt

½ tsp. ground black pepper

2 cups mushrooms, chopped

¼ cup yellow onion, minced

2 cloves garlic, minced

2 tbsp. fresh parsley, chopped

1 tsp. dried thyme

Directions:

1. Preheat the hair fryer to 325 degrees F. Brush the pork chops with half the olive oil and season with half of the salt and pepper. Place in the fryer basket and cook for 15 minutes.

2. While the pork chops cook, heat the remaining oil in a large skillet. Once hot, add the remaining ingredients and season with the remaining salt and pepper. Cook, about 10 minutes, until onions are soft.

3. Place 4 large sheets of aluminum foil on a flat surface. Remove the pork chops from the fryer and place in the center of each sheet. Top each pork chop with the mushroom mixture and wrap the mushroom topped pork chops with the foil.

4. Place the foil wrapped chops back in the air fryer and cook for 20 minutes.

5. Carefully open the foil before serving.

6. Enjoy!

Baby Back Ribs

(Total Time: 60 MIN | Serves: 4)

Ingredients:

1 tsp fresh ginger, grated

2 tbsp. yellow onion, minced

1 jalapeno, seeds and stem
    removed, chopped small

2 cloves garlic, minced

1 tbsp. fresh cilantro, chopped

1 tbsp. paprika

1 cup orange juice

2 tbsp. of sesame oil

¼ cup honey

1 full rack pork ribs

Directions:

1. In a large bowl, combine all ingredients except for ribs.

2. Place the ribs in a large Ziploc bag, pour half of the marinade mixture over the ribs. Close and refrigerate overnight. Reserve the remaining marinade in a sealed container and refrigerate.

3. Preheat air fryer to 365 degrees F. Remove the pork from the marinade and place in the fryer basket. Cook for 30 minutes. Discard the marinade the pork was in overnight.

4. Meanwhile, heat the reserved marinade on a small pot and bring to a simmer. Simmer for 30 minutes.

5. Remove the ribs from the fryer and brush with hot sauce.

6. Serve and enjoy.

Sausage Fettuccine

(Total Time: 25 MIN | Serves: 4)

Ingredients:

1 lb. fettuccine pasta

2 tbsp. olive oil

1 lb. ground Italian sausages

1 small yellow onion, minced

2 cloves garlic, minced

½ cup white wine

1 tsp. salt

½ tsp. ground black pepper

¼ cup grated parmesan cheese

2 tbsp. fresh parsley, chopped

Directions:

1. Preheat fryer to 370 degrees F. Place the sausage into large 1 tbsp. size chunks into the fryer basket and cook for 10 minutes.

2. Bring a large pot of water to a boil. Once boiling, add the pasta and cook for 10 minutes or until tender. Drain and set aside.

3. In a large skillet, heat the olive oil. Add the onion and garlic and cook for 3 to 5 minutes or until soft and fragrant. Add the white wine and simmer for 5 minutes. Season with salt and pepper.

4. Remove the sausage from the fryer and add to the onion mixture. Add the pasta to the onion mixture and toss.

5. Add the Parmesan cheese and toss all ingredients to coat.

6. Spoon the pasta into serving bowls and sprinkle with parsley.

7. Serve and enjoy!

Pineapple Ribs

(Total Time: 30 MIN | Serves: 4

Ingredients:

2 pounds Cut Spareribs, boiled
   for 15 minutes
8 ounces favorite Salad Dressing
½ tsp Onion Powder
1 tsp Garlic Powder
1 tbsp. Olive Oil
6 ounces canned Pineapple Juice
Salt and Pepper, to taste

Directions:

1. Preheat your Air Fryer to 350 degrees F.
2. Place the ribs in the Air Fryer.
3. Sprinkle with the garlic and onion powder, and drizzle the oil over.
4. Close the Air Fryer and cook for 15 minutes.
5. Whisk together the dressing and pineapple juice.
6. Add ¼ cup of this mixture in the Air Fryer and cook for 5 more minutes.
7. Serve the ribs alongside the remaining dressing and juice mixture.
8. Enjoy!

Ham and Onion Biscuits

Ingredients:

3 packages Pepperidge Farm Roll

1 pound Ham, chopped

1 tsp Mustard Seeds

1 Onion, diced

1 tbsp. Butter, softened

1 tsp Poppy Seeds

Pinch of Sea Salt

Pinch of Pepper

Directions:

1. Preheat your Air Fryer to 390 degrees F.
2. Mix the onion, poppy seeds, mustard seeds, butter, salt, and pepper, in a bowl.
3. Spread this mixture over the rolls.
4. Top with the ham.
5. Grease the Air Fryer with some cooking spray and arrange the biscuits in it.
6. Air Fry for 10 minutes.
7. Serve and enjoy!

Beef and Broccoli

(Total Time: 45 MIN | Serves: 4)

Ingredients:

1 pound of steak, sliced into strips

1 tbsp. of ginger, minced

1 tbsp. of soy sauce

1 pound of broccoli, stemmed and chopped

1 tbsp. of minced garlic

1 tbsp. of olive oil

1/3 cup of oyster sauce

1 tbsp. of sesame oil

1/3 cup of sherry

1 tsp of cornstarch

Directions:

1. Preheat the air fryer to 360 degrees Fahrenheit.
2. Combine the oyster sauce, soy sauce, sherry, olive oil, minced ginger, sesame oil, minced garlic, and cornstarch in a bowl.
3. Mix well and add the steak to it.
4. Add the broccoli and mix well. Let it marinate in the fridge for 30 minutes or overnight.
5. Add to your air fryer and cook for about 15 minutes.
6. Serve hot.

Air Fried Meatloaf

(Total Time: 25 MIN | Serves: 4)

Ingredients:

1 ½ pound of lean ground beef

1 finely chopped onion

1 tbsp. of chopped thyme

1 chopped green bell pepper

½ cup of chopped mushrooms

1/3 cup of steak sauce

1 tsp of paprika

1 tsp of salt

1 beaten egg

1 tsp of garlic powder

1 cup of panko breadcrumbs

1 tsp of black pepper

Directions:

1. Preheat the air fryer to 390 degrees Fahrenheit.
2. Combine the onion, thyme, bell pepper, mushrooms, steak sauce, salt, paprika, garlic powder, breadcrumbs, black pepper and egg.
3. Mix well and add the ground beef.
4. Mix again and add the mixture to your loaf pan.
5. Add to the air fryer and bake for about 25 minutes.
6. Serve warm.

Rib Eye-Steak

(Total Time: 20 MIN | Serves: 1 or 2)

Ingredients:

2 pounds of rib-eye steak

1 tsp of black pepper

1 tsp of mustard powder

1 tsp of ground coriander

1 tsp of salt

1 tsp of brown sugar

1 tsp of chili powder

1 tbsp. of olive oil

1 tsp of sweet paprika

1 tsp of onion powder

1 tsp of garlic powder

Directions:

1. Preheat the air fryer to 390 degrees Fahrenheit.
2. Combine all the spices in a bowl. Add the oil and mix well.
3. Coat the steak in the mixture nicely.
4. Add to the air fryer and cook for only 8 minutes.
5. Flip the steak and cook for additional 7 minutes.
6. Serve hot.

Zucchini Bacon Cheesy Lasagna

(Total Time: 30 MIN | Serves: 4)

Ingredients:

2 thinly sliced zucchinis

2 cups of grated mozzarella
cheese

1 tsp of garlic powder

2 tsp of onion powder

1 tsp of salt

6 strips of bacon

2 cups of grated ricotta cheese

1 tsp of black pepper

Cooking spray

Directions:

1. Preheat the air fryer to 390 degrees Fahrenheit.
2. Use a cooking spray to grease a lasagna pan.
3. Combine the onion powder, ricotta cheese, garlic powder, mozzarella cheese, salt, and pepper in a bowl.
4. Arrange the zucchini slices into your pan.
5. Add the cheese mix and top with bacon.
6. Again add a layer of cheese.
7. Repeat the process until you are left with nothing.
8. Add the pan to your air fryer.
9. Bake for 15 minutes and serve warm.

Poultry

Cheesy Chicken Spaghetti

(Total Time: 35 MIN | Serves: 6)

Ingredients:

4 (6oz) boneless skinless chicken breast, cut into 1in cubes

2 cups chicken broth

1 tbsp. butter

1 tsp. salt

1 tsp. ground black pepper

1 (1 lb.) package dry spaghetti

1 tbsp. olive oil

½ green pepper, diced small

1 medium yellow onion, diced small

2 cloves garlic, minced

1 cup fresh sliced mushrooms

2 (24oz) jars marinara sauce

1 cup ricotta cheese

2 cups shredded mozzarella cheese

¼ cup grated parmesan cheese

Directions:

1. Preheat the air fryer to 350 degrees F. Bring the chicken broth to a boil. Once boiling add the cubed chicken and boil for 10 minutes.

2. Drain the chicken. Coat the boiled chicken with the butter, salt and pepper. Place the chicken in the fryer basked and cook for 15 minutes.

3. Meanwhile, cook the spaghetti according to the package instructions.

4. Next, in a large skillet, heat the olive oil on medium heat. Once hot, add the green pepper, onion, garlic, and mushrooms. Cook until the vegetables are soft. Stir in the marinara sauce and bring to a simmer. Remove from heat and stir in the ricotta cheese.

5. Drain the cooked spaghetti and add to the sauce mixture. Stir to coat the noodles in the sauce. Once coated, spoon in to serving bowls.

6. Remove the chicken from the fryer. Place on top of the spaghetti. Sprinkle mozzarella and parmesan on top of the chicken. Serve and enjoy!

Chicken and Tomato Rice

(Total Time: 40 MIN | Serves: 4)

Ingredients:

4 chicken legs

3 tbsp. butter, melted

1 tsp. salt

½ tsp. ground black pepper

1 tbsp. Italian seasoning

2 cups chicken broth

1 cup white rice

1 tbsp. olive oil

1 small yellow onion, diced small

3 cloves garlic, minced

1 tbsp. tomato paste

1 (15oz) can diced tomatoes, drained

Directions:

1. Pre heat the air fryer to 360 degrees F.

2. Brush the chicken with the melted butter and season with the salt, pepper, and Italian seasoning. Place in the air fryer basket and cook for 30 minutes.

3. Sprinkle with salt and pepper and bake it in a preheated Air fryer for 35 minutes at 360° F.

4. While the chicken cooks, bring the chicken broth to a boil in a sauce pot. Once boiling add the rice and reduce to a simmer. Cover and simmer for 20 minutes or until the rice is tender and the broth is absorbed.

5. Heat the olive oil in a large skillet. Once hot, add the onion and garlic. Cook until the onions are softer. Stir in the tomato paste, and cook, stirring, for 2 minutes. Add the diced tomatoes and remove from heat.

6. Once cooked, add the rice to the tomato mixture and stir to coat the rice in the tomato sauce. Spoon the rice on to a serving plate.

7. Remove the chicken from the air fryer and place on top of rice.

8. Serve and enjoy!

Air Fried Turkey Breast

(Total Time: 45 MIN | Serves: 4)

Ingredients:

1 whole boneless and skinless
   turkey breast

¼ cup butter, melted

2 tsp. salt

1 tsp. ground black pepper

2 tbsp. dried parsley

1 tbsp. poultry seasoning

Directions:

1. Rinse and dry the chicken breast.
2. Combine the remaining ingredients and create a paste. Coat the turkey breast in the paste coating all sides. Lightly cover and refrigerate for one hour.
3. Preheat the air fryer to 370 degrees F.
4. Remove the turkey breast from the refrigerator and place in the air fryer basket. Cook for 20 minutes, turn the breast over, and cook for an additional 20 minutes.
5. Let rest for 10 minutes before slicing and serving
6. Serve and enjoy!

Chicken and Gravy Over Noodles

(Total Time: 35 MIN | Serves: 4)

Ingredients:

4 (6oz) boneless and skinless
   chicken breast

2 tbsp. butter, melted

2 tsp. salt

1 tsp. ground black pepper

1 tbsp. poultry seasoning

1 lb. uncooked egg noodles

2 cups chicken broth

2 tbsp. corn starch

2 tbsp. cold water

Directions:

1. Preheat the air fryer to 350 degrees F.
2. Coat the chicken in the butter, half the salt, half the pepper, and half the poultry seasoning. Place the coated chicken in the fryer basket and cook for 20 minutes.
3. Arrange the chicken breasts in the basket and set the timer to 20 minutes.
4. Meanwhile, cook the egg noodles according to the package.
5. Next, in a small sauce pan, bring the chicken broth to a boil with the remaining salt, pepper, and poultry seasoning. Once boiling, combine the corn starch and cold water in a small bowl. Gradually add the corn starch mixture to the boiling broth, stirring constantly until the mixture has thickened.
6. Drain the noodles and place on serving plates.
7. Remove the chicken from the air fryer and place on top of the noodles. Pour the gravy over top. Serve and enjoy!

Chicken and Tomato Risotto

(Total Time: 35 MIN | Serves: 4)

Ingredients:

8 oz boneless and skinless chicken
    breast, cubed

3 garlic cloves, minced

1 (14 oz) can diced tomatoes

¼ tsp cayenne pepper

1 tsp. ground turmeric

1 cup onion, minced

2 cups Arborio rice

4 cups chicken broth

1 tsp salt

2 tbsp. olive oil

2 tbsp. butter, melted

Directions:

1. Preheat fryer to 350 degrees F.
2. Coat the chicken in the butter and season with salt. Cook for 15 minutes. Remove and add the onions and garlic, cook for another 5 minutes.
3. Heat the olive oil in a skillet and add the rice cook just until browned. Stir in the tomatoes, turmeric, and cayenne. Add 1 cup of the broth and stir just until the broth is absorbed. Repeat with remaining broth.
4. Add the chicken mixture.
5. Serve and enjoy!

Chicken n' Biscuits

(Total Time: 45 MIN | Serves: 4)

Ingredients:

2 tbsp. flour

1 package chicken flavor gravy
   mix

1½ cups water

1 cup carrots, diced small

1 cup celery, diced small

1 cup yellow onion, diced small

1 tbsp. garlic powder

1 tsp. salt

½ tsp. ground black pepper

4 (6oz) boneless skinless chicken
   breast

1 tube refrigerated buttermilk
   biscuits

Directions:

1. Preheat the air fryer to 350 degrees F.
2. In a heat safe cooking bag, combine the flour and gravy mix and combine with the water. Close the bag tightly and shake to combine.
3. Open the bag, and place the carrots, celery, and onion in the gravy mixture. Sprinkle with some of the garlic powder, salt, and pepper.
4. Place the chicken on top of the vegetables, and season with the remaining garlic powder, salt and pepper.
5. Carefully arrange the biscuits around the chicken and securely tie the bag closed.
6. Place in the fryer basket and cook for 35 minutes.
7. Serve and enjoy!

Chicken and Cabbage Spring Rolls

(Total Time: 30 MIN | Serves: 4)

Ingredients:

1 Carrot, grated

½ medium Cabbage Head, sliced

1 package of Spring Roll
  Wrappers

1 tbsp. grated Ginger

1 tbsp. Oyster Sauce

½ pound Chicken Breast, diced

1 tbsp. Soy Sauce

2 tbsp. Corn Flour

1 tsp minced Garlic

1 Onion, diced

1 tbsp. Water

1 tbsp. Olive Oil

Pinch of Salt

Pinch of Pepper

Directions:

1. Preheat your Air Fryer to 340 degrees F.
2. In the Air Fryer add oil, carrot, cabbage, ginger, onion, garlic, oyster sauce, soy sauce, and chicken, and cook for 10 minutes.
3. Season with salt and pepper.
4. Divide the mixture between the spring roll wrappers.
5. Whisk together the corn flour and water.
6. Wrap the rolls and brush the corn paste over.
7. Grease the Air Fryer with cooking spray.
8. Arrange the spring rolls in the Air Fryer and cook for 10 minutes.
9. Serve and enjoy!

Basil and Garlic Chicken Legs

(Total Time: 30 MIN | Serves: 4)

Ingredients:

4 Chicken Legs

2 tbsp. Olive Oil

4 tsp dried Basil

2 tsp minced Garlic

Pinch of Pepper

Pinch of Salt

1 Lemon, sliced

Directions:

1. Preheat your Air Fryer to 350 degrees F.
2. Brush the chicken with the oil and sprinkle with the remaining ingredients.
3. Place in the Air Fryer and arrange the lemon slices around the chicken legs.
4. Close the lid and cook for 20 minutes.
5. Serve and enjoy!

Chicken Veggie Bake

(Total Time: 50 MIN | Serves: 4)

Ingredients:

1 pound Chicken Breasts, cubed

1 small Onion, chopped

1 Bell Pepper, diced

1 Carrot, chopped

1 tbsp. Sugar

3 tbsp. Soy Sauce

½ cup cashews, chopped

1 tbsp. Corn Flour

1 tsp minced Garlic

1 tbsp. Oyster Sauce

¼ tsp White Pepper

¼ tsp Salt

Directions:

1. In a bowl, place the chicken, soy sauce, oyster sauce, salt, pepper, and corn flour. Let marinate for 30 minutes in the fridge.
2. Preheat your Air Fryer to 390 degrees F.
3. Transfer the chicken to the Air Fryer along with the remaining ingredients.
4. Stir to combine.
5. Cook for 15 minutes.
6. Serve and enjoy!

Marjoram Chicken Breasts

(Total Time: 20 MIN | Serves: 2)

Ingredients:

1 large Chicken Breast

¼ cup chopped Marjoram

¼ tsp Garlic Powder

½ tbsp. Butter

¼ tsp Salt

Pinch of Pepper

Directions:

1. Preheat your Air Fryer to 390 degrees F.
2. Place the chicken on a piece of foil.
3. Sprinkle with salt, pepper, and garlic pepper.
4. Place the Marjoram on top.
5. Top with the butter.
6. Wrap the chicken in the foil.
7. Place in the Air Fryer and cook for 13 minutes.
8. Serve and enjoy!

Sweet and Lemony Stuffed Chicken

(Total Time: 100 MIN | Serves: 5)

Ingredients:

1 Whole Chicken
1 Apple, chopped
1 Zucchini, chopped
1 Red Onion, chopped
2 Garlic Cloves, chopped
2 tbsp. Olive Oil
1 tsp Thyme
2 Apricots, chopped
Pinch of Salt
Pinch of Pepper

Glaze:

Juice from 1 Lemon
7 ounces Honey
2 tbsp. Olive Oil
Pinch of White Pepper
Pinch of Salt

Directions:

1. Preheat your Air Fryer to 330 degrees F.
2. Place the onion, garlic, apricots, zucchini, apple, thyme, oil, salt, and pepper, in a bowl.
3. Stuff the chicken's cavity with this mixture, but do not pack tightly.
4. Place the chicken in your previously greased Air Fryer and cook for 30 minutes.
5. Whisk together all of the glaze ingredients and brush the mixture over the chicken.
6. Air Fry the chicken for 60 more minutes.
7. Serve and enjoy!

Garlic and Lime Chicken Breasts

(Total Time: 3 hours and 30 MIN | Serves: 2)

Ingredients:

1 tbsp. Olive Oil

¼ tsp Thyme

¼ tsp Cumin

¼ tsp Basil

2 tsp minced Garlic

1 tbsp. minced Cilantro

2 tbsp. Lime Juice

1 Green Onion, minced

2 Chicken Breasts, boneless and
 skinless

¼ tsp Salt

Pinch of Pepper

Directions:

1. Place all of the ingredients in a Ziploc bag.
2. Seal the bag and shake it to coat the chicken well.
3. Place in the fridge and leave to marinade for 3 hours.
4. Preheat your Air Fryer to 390 degrees F.
5. Grease it with some cooking spray.
6. Transfer the chicken to the Air Fryer and cook for 20 minutes.
7. Serve and enjoy!

Air Fried Cordon Bleu

(Total Time: 35 MIN | Serves: 4)

Ingredients:

3 tbsp. Flour

1 tsp Paprika

4 tbsp. Butter

1 tbsp. Cornstarch

4 Chicken Breasts

4 slices of Swiss Cheese

4 slices of Ham

½ cup White Wine

1 cup of Heavy Cream

1 tsp Chicken Bouillon Granules

Directions:

1. Preheat your Air Fryer to 390 degrees F.
2. Pound the chicken with a meat pounder and add a slice of ham and cheese in the center.
3. Fold the edges over the filling and secure with toothpicks.
4. Combine the flour and paprika and coat the chicken with it.
5. Melt 1 tbsp. of the butter, add the chicken, and cook for 15 minutes.
6. Remove the chicken from the Air Fryer.
7. Stir in the rest of the ingredients.
8. Cook for 10 minutes.
9. Return the chicken to the Air Fryer and continue cooking for another 20 minutes.
10. Serve the chicken topped with the sauce.
11. Enjoy!

Maple Glazed Turkey Breast

(Total Time: 45 MIN | Serves: 6)

Ingredients:

5-pound of a whole turkey breast

1 tsp of black pepper

1 tsp of paprika

1 tsp of dried thyme

¼ cup of maple syrup

1 tsp of dried parsley

1 tbsp. of olive oil

1 tsp of salt

1 tsp of dried oregano

2 tbsp. of Dijon mustard

1 tbsp. of melted unsalted butter

Directions:

1. Preheat the air fryer to 360 degrees Fahrenheit.
2. Take the turkey breast and brush it using olive oil.
3. Combine all the spices and herbs in a bowl.
4. Rub the turkey using the spice mixture generously.
5. Add the turkey breast to your preheated air fryer.
6. Cook for about 25 minutes.
7. Flip it to the other side and cook for another 15 minutes.
8. Take out of the air fryer.
9. Add the Dijon mustard, maple syrup and butter into the air fryer.
10. And cook for 5 minutes. Drizzle it onto the turkey and serve.

Jamaican Chicken Meatballs

(Total Time: 20 MIN | Serves: 4)

Ingredients:

2 boneless, skinless chicken
    breasts
1 tbsp. of dried basil
2 tsp of jerk paste
1 tbsp. of dried cumin
1 tsp of chili powder
1 tsp of black pepper
2 tbsp. of honey
1 onion, peeled and chopped
1 tbsp. of dried thyme
1 tbsp. of mustard powder
1 tsp of salt
3 tbsp. of soy sauce

Directions:

1. Preheat the air fryer to 360 degrees Fahrenheit.
2. In a blender add the chicken breasts. Blend until it becomes minced.
3. Add the onion, herbs and the remaining ingredients.
4. Blend for 2 minutes.
5. Transfer the mixture into a bowl and create meatballs.
6. Fry the meatballs for about 15 minutes.
7. Serve hot.

Air-Fried Ravioli

🕒   🍽️

(Total Time: 10 MIN | Serves: 6)

Ingredients:

1 jar of marinara sauce

1 cup of buttermilk

1 tbsp. of olive oil

1 box of ravioli

2 cups of breadcrumbs

Directions:

1. Arrange the breadcrumbs in a plate.
2. Add the buttermilk in a bowl.
3. Take the ravioli and add to the buttermilk.
4. Coat them in the breadcrumbs.
5. Fry them in the Air fryer with 200 degrees Fahrenheit for 5 minutes.
6. Serve hot with the marinara sauce.

Air Fried Mac 'n Cheese

(Total Time: 40 MIN | Serves: 20)

Ingredients:

½ pound elbow macaroni pasta, cooked

½ cup cheddar cheese, grated

½ cup Fontina cheese, grated

½ cup Gruyere cheese, grated

½ cup heavy cream

½ cup milk

½ tsp salt

⅛ tsp ground nutmeg

¼ tsp black pepper

¼ cup Parmesan cheese, grated

¼ cup breadcrumbs

1 tbsp. butter, melted

Directions:

1. In a pan over very low heat, stir in the milk, heavy cream, cheddar, fontina, gruyere, salt, pepper, nutmeg, and pasta.
2. Let it simmer for 3-5 minutes.
3. Meanwhile, combine the breadcrumbs, parmesan, and butter together in a small bowl. Pour it into the cream mixture once it simmers.
4. Transfer the pasta mixture in a heat-proof bowl or dish. Place the dish in a preheated air fryer at 350°F and cook for half an hour.

Chicken on Olives and Prunes

(Total Time: MIN | Serves: 4)

Ingredients:

A handful of Green Olives

½ cup Prunes, pitted

3 Garlic Cloves, minced

¼ cup White Wine

1 tbsp. chopped Parsley

2 tbsp. Olive Oil

1 tbsp. Oregano

2 tbsp. Capers

1 Whole chicken

1 tbsp. Brown Sugar

2 tbsp. Red Wine Vinegar

Salt and Pepper, to taste

Directions:

1. Preheat your Air Fryer to 350 degrees F.
2. In a baking dish, combine all of the ingredients except the chicken, salt pepper, and sugar.
3. Season the chicken with some salt and pepper and place it on top of the olive and prune mixture.
4. Sprinkle with the brown sugar.
5. Cook for 60 minutes.
6. Serve and enjoy!

Turkey Tortilla Rolls

(Total Time: 20 MIN | Serves: 4)

Ingredients:

4 tortilla wraps

2 eggs

2 cups of leftover turkey breast, shredded

1 tbsp. of soy sauce

1 tsp of Worcester sauce

1 tbsp. of honey

1 tsp of salt

1 tsp of black pepper

1 tbsp. of Chinese five-spice

Directions:

1. Whisk the eggs in a bowl.
2. Shred the turkey breasts finely.
3. Add all the ingredients except the tortilla wraps.
4. Arrange the tortilla wraps on a flat surface.
5. Fill the middle using the turkey mixture.
6. Roll out the tortilla and brush the top using the egg wash.
7. Repeat the same with all the wraps.
8. Add to the air fryer and fry for about 5 minutes on 360 degrees Fahrenheit.
9. Serve hot.

Fresh Rosemary Chicken

(Total Time: 60 MIN | Serves: 4)

Ingredients:

1 Whole Chicken, cut into pieces

½ cup Olive Oil

½ cup White Wine

3 Garlic Cloves, chopped

2 tbsp. chopped Rosemary

2 Lemons, quartered

Salt and Pepper, to taste

Directions:

1. Preheat your Air Fryer to 350 degrees F.
2. Place all of the ingredients in your air Fryer and stir to combine.
3. Season with some salt and pepper, to taste.
4. Close the lid and Air Fry for 50 minutes.
5. Serve the chicken topped with the cooking juices.
6. Enjoy!

Chicken Thighs with Rice and Broccoli

(Total Time: 50 MIN | Serves: 4)

Ingredients:

1 cup chopped Broccoli

1 cup uncooked Rice

1 can Cream of Chicken Soup

3 Garlic Cloves, minced

2 cups Water

¼ tsp Garlic Powder

¼ tsp Salt

Pinch of Pepper

4 large Chicken Thighs

Directions:

1. Preheat your Air Fryer to 350 degrees F.
2. Grease the Air Fryer with cooking spray.
3. Arrange the chicken thighs inside and sprinkle with salt, pepper, and garlic powder.
4. Cook for 15 minutes. Transfer on a plate.
5. Combine the rest of the ingredients in the Air Fryer.
6. Add the chicken on top and cook for 30 more minutes.
7. Serve and enjoy!

Chicken Kebabs

(Total Time: 15 MIN | Serves: 2)

Ingredients:

2 chicken breasts, chopped
    boneless, skinless
1 red bell pepper, chopped
1/3 cup of soy sauce
1 tsp of black pepper
6 mushrooms, cut into half
1 green bell pepper, chopped
1/3 cup of honey
1 tsp of salt
1 yellow bell pepper, chopped
Wooden skewers

Directions:

1. Preheat the air fryer to 340 degrees Fahrenheit.
2. Combine the honey, salt, soy sauce and pepper in a bowl.
3. Mix well and set aside for now.
4. Use the skewers to thread the peppers, chicken and mushrooms.
5. Brush them using the honey mixture.
6. Add to the air fryer and cook for about 15 minutes.
7. Serve hot.

Indian-Style Chicken

(Total Time: 40 MIN | Serves: 2)

Ingredients:

½ pound Chicken Breast,
 chopped

2 tbsp. Olive Oil

2 Tomatoes, chopped

1 Onion, chopped

1 tbsp. Cumin

3 Green Peppers, chopped

3 Garlic Cloves, minced

1 tbsp. Mustard

1 tsp grated Ginger

Pinch of Coriander

Directions:

1. Preheat your Air Fryer to 360 degrees F.
2. Place everything except for the chicken, in your Air Fryer.
3. Cook for 5 minutes.
4. Add chicken and cook for additional 30 minutes, until really tender.
5. Serve and enjoy!

Asian Air Fried Chicken

(Total Time: 30 MIN | Serves: 6)

Ingredients:

½ cup Water

½ cup Sugar

2 tbsp. Soy Sauce

½ cup chopped Green Onion

4 tsp Sesame Oil

½ cup Olive Oil

¼ cup Cornstarch

2 pounds of Chicken Breasts, cut
   into pieces

6 tbsp. Flour

1 tsp Baking Powder

2 tbsp. grated Ginger

¼ cup Oyster Sauce

Directions:

1. Preheat your Air Fryer to 390 degrees F.
2. Coat the chicken with the cornstarch.
3. In a bowl whisk together the eggs and flour.
4. Dip the chicken in the batter,
5. Add the oil in the Air Fryer and arrange the battered chicken inside.
6. Cook for 5 minutes per side.
7. Stir in the remaining ingredients.
8. Stir well to coat the chicken.
9. Close the lid again and cook for another 20 minutes.
10. Serve and enjoy!

Sherry and Marsala Chicken

(Total Time: 35 MIN | Serves: 4)

Ingredients:

1 tbsp. Olive Oil

4 tbsp. Butter

¼ cup Flour

1 cup Sherry

5 Chicken Breasts

1 cup of sliced Mushrooms

¼ tsp Salt

Pinch of Pepper

¼ tsp Garlic Powder

Directions:

1. Preheat your Air Fryer to 350 degrees F.
2. Combine the flour, garlic powder, pepper, and salt, in a bowl.
3. Coat the chicken with the mixture.
4. Add the oil in the Air Fryer and arrange the chicken in it.
5. Cook for 12 minutes.
6. Stir in the remaining ingredients.
7. Close the lid and continue cooking for another 10 minutes.
8. Serve and enjoy!

Chicken on Skewers

(Total Time: 20 MIN | Serves: 5)

Ingredients:

1 ½ pound Chicken Breasts, cut into pieces

Zest of 2 Lemons

3 tbsp. Olive Oil

Salt and Pepper, to taste

½ tsp Garlic Powder

Directions:

1. Preheat your Air Fryer to 350 degrees F.
2. Season the chicken with salt, pepper, and garlic powder.
3. Thread the chicken onto 20 skewers.
4. Place in the Air Fryer (you may need to work in batches).
5. Combine the olive oil and zest and drizzle the mixture over the chicken.
6. Close the lid and cook for 12 minutes.
7. Serve and enjoy!

Chicken Nuggets

(Total Time: 20 MIN | Serves: 4)

Ingredients:

1 pound of chicken breasts,
    boneless, skinless
1 cup of breadcrumbs
1 cup of milk
2 tsp of salt
2 cups of flour
1 tsp of black pepper
1 beaten egg
1 tsp of sweet paprika

Directions:

1. Preheat the air fryer to 360 degrees Fahrenheit.
2. Cut the chicken into 1 inch cubes.
3. Whish the eggs with the milk.
4. Add the flour in a plate and set aside for now.
5. Combine breadcrumbs, sweet paprika, salt and pepper in another bowl.
6. Toss the chicken in the flour and then dip in the whisked egg mix.
7. Toss in the breadcrumbs mix and add to the air fryer.
8. Air fry for about 10 minutes and serve hot.

Pineapple BBQ Chicken Kebabs

(Total Time: 20 MIN | Serves: 2)

Ingredients:

2 Bell Peppers, chopped into
large pieces

½ Onion, chopped into large
pieces

½ pound Chicken Breasts,
chopped

¼ cup Barbecue Sauce

¼ tsp Garlic Salt

Pinch of Pepper

1 can Pineapple Chunks

Directions:

1. Preheat your Air Fryer to 390 degrees F.
2. Thread the chicken, bell pepper, onion, and pineapple onto 6 skewers.
3. Sprinkle with pepper and garlic salt.
4. Brush with barbecue sauce.
5. Grease the Air Fryer with cooking spray.
6. Arrange the skewers in the Air Fryer.
7. Cook for 10 minutes.
8. Serve and enjoy!
9.

Seafood

Seafood Spaghetti

(Total Time: 25 MIN | Serves: 4)

Ingredients:

1 tbsp. olive oil

1 tbsp. butter melted

½ cup onion, diced

2 cloves garlic, minced

2 (15oz) cans diced tomatoes

1 lb. dry spaghetti

1 (4oz) can clams, drained

1 (8oz) can lump crab

1 cup mini shrimp, peeled, deveined, tails off

2 tbsp. dry parsley

Directions:

1. Preheat fryer to 350 degrees.

2. Drizzle the shrimp, crab, and clams with melted butter. Place in fryer basket and cook for 5 minutes. Remove from fryer and set aside.

3. Bring a pot of water to a boil. Add the spaghetti and cook for 10 minutes or until tender.

4. Heat the olive oil in a skillet. Once hot add the onion and garlic. Cook until soft. Stir in the tomatoes. Stir in the cooked seafood.

5. Drain the pasta and add to the seafood and tomatoes. Toss to coat.

6. Serve and enjoy!

Coconut Fried Shrimp

(Total Time: 15 MIN | Serves: 4)

Ingredients:

½ cup water

½ tsp baking powder

1 tbsp. corn starch

1 tsp salt

½ cup flour

1 cup shredded unsweetened
coconut

½ cup Panko bread crumbs

1 lb. raw, large, peeled and
deveined shrimp

1 tbsp. olive oil

¼ cup honey

Directions:

1. Preheat the air fryer to 390 degrees F.
2. In a small bowl, whisk together the water, baking powder, cornstarch, salt, and flour. Whisk until smooth. Let sit for 10 minutes.
3. In a food processor, combine the coconut and Panko. Pulse until the crumbs are very fine. Transfer the mixture to a second small bowl.
4. Dip the shrimp in the flour batter, and then dip the shrimp in the coconut mixture making sure the shrimp are coated each time.
5. Place the coated shrimp in the fryer basket and drizzle with oil, cook for 3 minutes.
6. Remove the shrimp once cooked and drizzle with olive oil.
7. Serve and enjoy.

Salmon Risotto

(Total Time: 25 MIN | Serves: 4)

Ingredients:

8 oz. salmon, cut into small
  chunks

2 garlic cloves, minced

½ cup onion, chopped

1 cup of Arborio rice

1 tbsp. olive oil

½ cup peas

2 cups chicken broth, warm

2 tbsp. butter, melted

1 tsp salt

½ tsp ground pepper

Directions:

1. Preheat fryer to 320 degrees F.
2. Coat the salmon in the butter, onions and garlic and season with salt and pepper. Cook for 10 minutes
3. Heat the oil in a large skillet and add the rice. Cook until lightly browned. Add 1 cup of the chicken broth and stir until absorbed. Repeat until all the broth is used.
4. Stir in the peas and salmon mixture.
5. Serve and enjoy!

Shrimp and Mushroom Risotto

(Total Time: 30 MIN | Serves: 3)

Ingredients:

4 cups vegetable broth

2 tbsp. olive oil

4 tbsp. butter, melted

2 small shallots, minced

2 cloves garlic, minced

4 cups sliced mushrooms

2 cups Arborio rice

½ cup of dry white wine

½ cup parmesan cheese

2 cups small shrimp, peeled, deveined, tails removed

Directions:

1. Preheat the air fryer to 320 degrees F.
2. Rinse the rice and place in the fryer. Cook for 5 minutes. Add the shallots, garlic, and mushrooms. Drizzle with the melted butter. Cooke for 8 more minutes.
3. In a skillet, heat the olive oil. Add the shrimp cook for two minutes and add wine. Remove the rice mixture from the air fryer and add to the wine. Stir to combine. Cook just until the wine is absorbed.
4. Add 1 cup of the broth. Cook until the broth is absorbed. Repeat until all the broth has been used. Stir in the parmesan cheese.
5. Serve and enjoy!

Salmon Quiche

(Total Time: 60 MIN | Serves: 4)

Ingredients:

2 cups salmon, skinless and
   cubed

1 tsp. salt

¼ tsp. ground black pepper

1 (9 in) premade pie crust

¼ cup green onion, chopped

½ cup shredded mozzarella
   cheese

4 tbsp. heavy cream

3 large eggs

1 tbsp. Dijon mustard

Directions:

1. Preheat the air fryer to 350 degrees F
2. Season the salmon with salt and pepper. Set aside
3. Place the premade pie crust into individual quiche pans and press into the sides of the pans. Trim off any overhanging crust.
4. Trim the dough onto the edges of the pan you intend to use or just let it stick out.
5. Place the cubed salmon into the crust and top with the green onion and mozzarella.
6. In a mixing bowl, combine the heavy cream, eggs, and mustard. Carefully pour over the salmon being careful not cause the mixture to over flow.
7. Carefully slide the quiche into the fryer basket and cook for 20 minutes.
8. Let rest for 10 minutes before serving.
9. Enjoy!

Air Fried Catfish

(Total Time: 20 MIN | Serves: 4)

Ingredients:

4 large catfish filets

1 tsp. salt

½ tsp. ground black pepper

2 eggs, lightly beaten

½ cup Panko bread crumbs

½ cup flour

2 tbsp. Cajun seasoning

1 tbsp. olive oil

1 tbsp. lemon juice

Directions:

1. Preheat the air fryer to 340 degrees F.
2. Season the catfish with salt and pepper and set aside.
3. Place the beaten eggs in a small bowl.
4. Place the panko, flour, and Cajun seasoning in a food processor and gently pulse until the panko crumbs are fine. Transfer the mixture to a second small bowl.
5. Dip each catfish filet in to the panko and flour mixture. Then, place the fish into the eggs. Last, dip the catfish in to the panko and flour mixture one more time. Ensure all sides of the fish are coated.
6. Place the fish into the fryer basket and cook for 15 minutes. Remove from the fryer and drizzle with lemon juice.
7. Serve and enjoy!

Cedar Plank Salmon

(Total Time: 30 MIN | Serves: 6)

Ingredients:

4 untreated cedar planks

1½ tbsp. of rice vinegar

2 tbsp. sesame oil

½ cup soy sauce

¼ cup green onions, chopped

3 cloves garlic, minced

1 tbsp. fresh ginger grated

2 lb. of salmon fillets, skin removed

Directions:

1. Submerge the cedar planks in water and soak for 2 hours.
2. In a shallow dish, combine all ingredients except salmon and mix well.
3. Add the salmon to the marinade and coat each side. Marinate, refrigerated, for 30minutes.
4. Preheat fryer to 350 degrees F.
5. Remove the cedar planks from the water and pat dry. Place on the fryer basket and place the salmon on top
6. Cook for 15 minutes.
7. Serve and enjoy

Halibut Sitka

(Total Time: 20 MIN | Serves: 6)

Ingredients:

6 (8 oz) skinless halibut filets

1 tsp. salt

½ tsp. ground black pepper

½ cup green onion, chopped

½ cup mayonnaise

½ cup sour cream

1 tsp. dry dill

Directions:

1. Preheat the air fryer to 390 degrees F
2. Season the halibut with salt and pepper, place on the fryer plate.
3. In a small bowl, combine the remaining ingredients. Mix well then spread over the top of the halibut.
4. Cook for 15 minutes.
5. Serve and enjoy!

Air Fried Calamari and Tomato Pasta

(Total Time: 25 MIN | Serves: 4)

Ingredients:

2 cloves garlic, minced

1 lb. sliced calamari, cut into rings

1 egg

1 cup Italian bread crumbs

1 tbsp. of olive oil

½ cup diced onion

2 tsp Italian seasoning

2 (15 oz) cans diced tomatoes, drained

1 lb. dry angel hair pasta

½ cup grated parmesan

Directions:

1. Preheat fryer to 360 degrees.
2. Dip the calamari into the egg and then into the bread crumbs. Coating all sides. Place in the air fryer basket and drizzle with olive oil. Cook for 15 minutes.
3. Meanwhile, bring a large pot of water to a boil. Add the pasta and cook for 10 minutes or until tender. Drain.
4. Combine the pasta, garlic, onion, Italian seasoning, and diced tomatoes. Heat just until hot. Spoon on to a serving plate.
5. Remove calamari from air fryer and place on top of pasta. Sprinkle with parmesan.
6. Serve and enjoy!

Air Fried Chili Octopus

(Total Time: 35 MIN | Serves: 3)

Ingredients:

7 medium green chilies, diced
   small

2 cloves garlic, minced

1 tsp salt

2 tbsp. lime juice

¼ tsp. ground black pepper

1 tbsp. sugar

2 tbsp. olive oil

1 lb. of clean octopus, cut into
   bite sized cubes

1 tsp fish sauce

1 tsp. soy sauce

1 tbsp. fresh cilantro, finely
   chopped

Directions:

1. Preheat air fryer to 370 degrees F.

2. Season the octopus with salt, and arrange in the air fryer basket. Drizzle with 1 tbsp. of the olive oil. Cook for 4 minutes. The remove and turn the octopus over and cook 4 more minutes.

3. While the octopus cooks, combine the remaining ingredients in a small bowl. Mix well to create a sauce.

4. Remove the octopus from the fryer and serve with the dipping sauce on the side. Enjoy!

Air Fried Dragon Shrimp

(Total Time: 15 MIN | Serves: 4)

Ingredients:

1 lb raw shrimp, peeled and
   deveined

2 eggs

2 tbsp. olive oil

½ cup soy sauce

1 cup yellow onion, diced

½ tsp ground ginger

½ tsp salt

¼ cup flour

½ tsp ground red pepper

Directions:

1. Preheat air fryer to 350 degrees F.
2. Combine all ingredients, except for the shrimp, and create a batter. Let sit for 10 minutes.
3. Dip the shrimp into the batter to coat all sides and place in the fryer basket.
4. Cook for 10 minutes and serve.
5. Enjoy!

Chinese Mushroom Tilapia

(Total Time: 20 MIN | Serves: 4)

Ingredients:

4 (8oz) filets tilapia

2½ tsp of salt

2 tbsp. olive oil

2 cups sliced mushrooms

½ cup yellow onion, sliced thin

2 cloves garlic, minced

4 tbsp. soy sauce

1 tsp. red chili flakes

1 tbsp. honey

2 tbsp. rice vinegar

Directions:

1. Preheat the fryer to 350 degrees F.
2. Season the fish with half the salt and drizzle with half the oil. Cook for 15 minutes.
3. Meanwhile, heat the remaining oil in a large skillet. Once hot add the mushroom onion, and garlic. Cook until onions are soft.
4. Stir in the soy sauce, chili flakes, honey and vinegar. Simmer for 1 minute.
5. Remove fish from the fryer and top with mushroom sauce.
6. Serve and enjoy!

Air Fried Spinach Fish

(Total Time: 20 MIN | Serves: 4)

Ingredients:

1 cup spinach leaves, wilted

2 cups flour

1 tsp. salt

½ tsp. ground black pepper

2 tbsp. olive oil

1 large egg

4 (6oz) filets perch

1 tbsp. lemon juice

Directions:

1. Preheat the fryer to 370 degrees F.
2. In a bowl, combine the spinach, flour, salt, pepper, and egg.
3. Dip each filet in the batter and place on the fryer tray. Drizzle with olive oil.
4. Cook for 12 minutes. Remove and drizzle with lemon juice.
5. Serve and enjoy.

Fish Lettuce Wraps

(Total Time: 20 MIN | Serves: 3)

Ingredients:

6 iceberg lettuce leaves

6 small filets of tilapia

1 tsp salt

½ tsp ground black pepper

2 tsp. Cajun seasoning

1 tbsp. olive oil

½ cup shredded purple cabbage

½ cup shredded carrot

1 tbsp. lemon juice

Directions:

1. Preheat the air fryer to 390 degrees F.

2. Season tilapia with salt, pepper and Cajun seasoning. Drizzle with olive oil and place in the air fryer. Cook for 10 minutes.

3. Remove fish from the fryer and place the fish on each lettuce leaf. Top with carrots and cabbage.

4. Drizzle lemon juice on top, serve and enjoy!

Tuna Risotto

(Total Time: 35 MIN | Serves: 6)

Ingredients:

1 tbsp. olive oil

2 cups Arborio rice

½ cup yellow onion, minced

4 cups chicken broth, warm

¼ cup grated parmesan cheese

1 cup peas

2 (4oz) cans tuna, drained

1 tsp. ground black pepper

Directions:

1. Preheat air fryer to 320.
2. Season the tuna and peas with black pepper. Place in the air fryer and cook for 10 minutes.
3. Meanwhile, heat the oil and add the onion and rice. Cook until lightly browned.
4. Add 1 cup of the warm broth, and cook until absorbed. Repeat until all the broth is used.
5. Stir in the parmesan, tuna, and peas.
6. Serve and enjoy!

Air Fried Perch

(Total Time: 20 MIN | Serves: 5)

Ingredients:

5 perch filets

1 tsp. salt

1 cup buttermilk

2 tbsp. olive oil

1 cup flour

2 tsp. garlic powder

2 tsp. paprika

1 tbsp. chili powder

Directions:

1. Combine the salt, flour, garlic, paprika, and chili powder. Stir until combined.
2. Dip the perch in to the flour mixture, then into the buttermilk, and then back into the flour making sure to coat all sides.
3. Place in the fryer basket and drizzle with oil. Cook for 10 minutes.
4. Serve and enjoy!

Shrimp Spaghetti

(Total Time: 20 MIN | Serves: 4)

Ingredients:

1 lb. dry spaghetti

4 cups small shrimp, peeled, deveined, tails removed

4 cloves garlic, minced

1 tsp. salt

½ tsp. crushed red pepper

3 tbsp. olive oil

1 tbsp. butter, melted

1 tbsp. dry basil

3 tsp. dry oregano

½ cup grated parmesan

Directions:

1. Preheat fryer to 390 degrees.
2. Toss the shrimp with the salt, half the red pepper, butter, and 1 tbsp. of the oil. Place in the fry basket and cook for 5 minutes.
3. Bring a large pot of water to a boil, once boiling add the pasta. Cook for 10 minutes or until tender.
4. Drain the pasta and add the remaining ingredients. Remove the shrimp and add to the pasta. Toss to combine well.
5. Serve and enjoy!

Prawn Curry

(Total Time: 15 MIN | Serves: 4)

Ingredients:

6 king prawns

1 tsp salt

½ tsp ground black pepper

1 tbsp. olive oil

2 tbsp. curry powder

1 medium finely chopped onion

1½ cup chicken broth

½ tsp of coriander

1 tbsp. tomato paste

Directions:

1. Preheat the air fryer to 370 degrees F.
2. Season the prawns with salt and pepper. Cook for 7 minutes.
3. Meanwhile, heat the olive oil in a large skillet. Once hot add the onion. Cook until soft. Sit in the curry, tomato paste, and coriander.
4. Cook, stirring, for 1 minutes. Add the chicken broth and stir until smooth.
5. Remove prawns from the fryer and add to the sauce.
6. Serve and enjoy!

Asian Tilapia

(Total Time: 60 MIN | Serves: 4)

Ingredients:

1 tsp. salt

½ tsp. ground black pepper

1 tbsp. ground turmeric

½ tsp. chili powder

1 tsp. garlic powder

¾ tsp. ginger

½ tsp. ground cumin

4 tilapia filet

1 tbsp. sesame oil

Directions:

1. Preheat the air fryer to 340 degrees F.
2. Combine the salt, pepper, turmeric, chili powder, garlic powder, ginger, and cumin. Sprinkle the spices on to the tilapia.
3. Place the tilapia in to the fryer basket and drizzle with sesame oil. Bake for 12 minutes.
4. Serve and enjoy!

Tandori Fish

(Total Time: 25 MIN | Serves: 4)

Ingredients:

1 whole fish, such as trout

1 tbsp. Garam Masala seasoning

3 tbsp. olive oil

8 cloves garlic, minced

1 cup papaya, mashed

1 tsp. ground turmeric

½ tsp. ground cumin

1 tbsp. chili powder

1 tsp. salt

½ tsp. ground black pepper

Directions:

1. Preheat the air fryer to 340 degrees F. Slash slits into the sides of the fish.

2. Combine all remaining ingredients and coat all sides of the fish with the mixture.

3. Place the coated fish into the fryer basket and cook for 20 minutes.

4. Serve and enjoy!

Pecan Crusted Salmon

(Total Time: 20 MIN | Serves: 4)

Ingredients:

3 tbsp. Dijon mustard

3 tbsp. olive oil

1 tbsp. honey

½ cup Panko bread crumbs

½ cup pecans

3 tbsp. fresh chopped parsley

1 tsp. salt

½ tsp. ground black pepper

4 salmon filets

1 tbsp. lemon juice

Directions:

1. Preheat air fryer to 390 degrees F.

2. In a small bowl combine the mustard, oil, and honey.

3. Combine the Panko, pecans, parsley, salt, and pepper in a food processor and process until crumbs are fine.

4. Dip the salmon in the mustard mixture then dip the salmon into the pecan mixture, pressing the pecans into all sides of the fish.

5. Place the coated salmon in the fryer basket and cook for 10 minutes. Drizzle with lemon juice.

6. Serve and enjoy!

Crusted Halibut

(Total Time: 30 MIN | Serves: 4)

Ingredients:

¾ cup Panko bread crumbs

½ cup fresh parsley, chopped

¼ cup fresh dill, chopped

2 tsp. lemon zest

1 tsp. salt

½ tsp. ground black pepper

4 halibut filets

1 tbsp. olive oil

Directions:

1. Preheat the air fryer to 390 degrees F.

2. Combine all ingredients except halibut and olive oil in a food processor and pulse until the mixture is a fine crumb.

3. Gently coat the halibut in the mixture and place inside the fryer basket. Drizzle with olive oil and cook for 25 minutes.

4. Serve and enjoy!

Cheesy Bacon Wrapped Shrimp

(Total Time: 20 MIN | Serves: 4)

Ingredients:

16 extra large raw shrimp, peeled, deveined, and butter flied
16 (1 in) cubes cheddar jack cheese
16 slices of bacon, cooked half way
¼ cup BBQ sauce

Directions:

1. Preheat the air fryer to 350 degrees F.
2. Stuff each shrimp with a cheese cube and wrap with a slice of bacon. Secure the bacon to the shrimp with a tooth pick.
3. Brush the wrapped shrimp with BBQ sauce and place in the air fryer. Cook for 6 minutes.
4. Remove and brush with additional BBQ sauce.
5. Serve and enjoy!

Crab Cakes

(Total Time: 20 MIN | Serves: 4)

Ingredients:

2 (6oz) cans crab meat

2 tbsp. yellow onion, minced

2 tbsp. red pepper, minced

2 tbsp. celery, minced

2 tbsp. Dijon mustard

2 tbsp. butter, melted

1 tsp. lemon juice

1 large egg, beaten

1 cup Panko bread crumbs

1 tsp. Worcestershire sauce

1 tsp Old Bay seasoning

Directions:

1. Preheat air fryer to 390 degrees F.
2. Combine all ingredients in a large bowl and mix well.
3. Form the mixture in to patties, about ¼ cup per patty. Carefully place each into the fryer basket.
4. Cook for 10 minutes. The patties may need to be cooked in batches.
5. Serve and enjoy!

Tuna with Fusilli Pasta

(Total Time: 20 MIN | Serves: 4)

Ingredients:

2 tbsp. olive oil

1 (15oz) can diced tomatoes, drained

½ tsp crushed red pepper

½ lemon, zested

1 lb. of Fusilli pasta, cooked

1 (4 oz.) can tuna, drained

½ cup shredded cheddar cheese

Directions:

1. Preheat fryer to 350 degrees F.
2. Combine all ingredients except for cheese. Mix well.
3. Place the mixture onto the fryer tray. Top with cheddar cheese.
4. Cook for 10 minutes. Remove from the fryer and serve
5. Enjoy!

Chinese Fried White Fish

(Total Time: 20 MIN | Serves: 4)

Ingredients:

1 lb. white fish

¼ tsp. ground ginger

¼ cup yellow onion, minced

½ tsp. salt

¼ tsp. ground black pepper

2 cloves garlic, minced

¼ tsp. Chinese five spice

1 tbsp. honey

1 tbsp. olive oil

Directions:

1. Combine all ingredients, except for the fish, and create a paste. Coat the fish in the past on all sides and refrigerate for 2 hours.
2. Preheat oven to 370 degrees F.
3. Remove the fish from the refrigerator and place in the fry basket. Cook for 15 minutes.
4. Serve and enjoy!

Salmon and Dill Bites

(Total Time: 15 MIN | Serves: 2)

Ingredients:

1 tbsp. chopped Dill

6 ounces canned Salmon

4 tbsp. chopped Celery

1 Egg

½ tsp Garlic Powder

5 tbsp. Wheat Germ

3 tbsp. Olive Oil

4 tbsp. Spring Onion, chopped

Pinch of Salt

Directions:

1. Preheat your Air Fryer to 370 degrees F.
2. Place the salmon, dill, egg, celery, spring onion, garlic powder, and salt, in a bowl.
3. Mix with your hands to combine. Shape the mixture into bite-sized balls.
4. Heat the oil in the Air Fryer.
5. Arrange the salmon balls in it.
6. Close the Air Fryer and cook for 10 minutes.
7. Serve and enjoy!

Cayenne Tuna Puffs

(Total Time: 25 MIN | Serves: 2)

Ingredients:

1 sheet of Puff Pastry

½ can Tuna, drained

Pinch of Cayenne Pepper

Directions:

1. Preheat your Air Fryer to 390 degrees F.
2. Cut the puff pastry into 4 equal pieces.
3. Divide the tuna between the pastry squares.
4. Fold the pastry and seal the edges with a fork.
5. Grease the Air Fryer with some cooking spray.
6. Arrange the stuffed pastry in it.
7. Air Fry for 15 minutes.
8. Serve and enjoy!

Sides

French Bread

(Total Time: 50 MIN | Serves: 7)

Ingredients:

6 cups flour

2 tbsp. active dry yeast

2 tbsp. sugar

1 tbsp. salt

1 tbsp. butter, melted

2 ½ cups warm water

Directions:

1. Combine water, yeast, and sugar in a large bowl. Mix until yeast is completely dissolved and let sit for 2 minutes.

2. Add in the remaining ingredients and mix until well combined. Knead the dough on a lightly floured surface until the dough is smooth and elastic.

3. Oil a clean, large bowl and place the dough inside. Cover and let rest for about an hour or until doubled.

4. Once doubled, shape the dough in to two loaves. Place on the fryer tray and let rest again for about 30 minutes or until doubled.

5. Preheat the fryer to 375. Bake for 25 minutes or until golden.

6. Enjoy!

Onion Beer Bread

(Total Time: 55 MIN | Serves: 5)

Ingredients:

3 cups self-rising flour

3 tbsp. sugar

1 egg

2 cups dark beer

1 large onion, chopped

2 tbsp. butter

Directions:

1. In a skillet, heat the butter. Once melted, add the onions and cook until lightly browned and soft. About 15 minutes.
2. Preheat fryer to 325 degrees F.
3. Combine the onions with all the ingredients and mix well. Knead the dough on a lightly floured surface until smooth and elastic.
4. Form into a loaf and place on the fryer tray. Pace for 40 minutes.
5. Enjoy!

Roasted Vegetable Rice

(Total Time: 35 MIN | Serves: 4)

Ingredients:

3 cups water

1 ½ cups brown rice

2 tbsp. peanut oil

1 cup yellow onion, cut large

1 cup green pepper, cut large

2 cloves garlic, minced

2 large tomatoes, cut into large cubes

2 cups carrots, cut large

2 tbsp. olive oil

1 tsp. salt

Directions:

1. Preheat fryer to 350 degrees F.
2. Coat the onion, pepper, garlic, tomatoes, and carrots in the peanut oil. Cook for 30 minutes.
3. Meanwhile, bring the water to a boil and add the rice. Reduce to a simmer and cook for 20 minutes or until water is absorbed and rice is tender.
4. Stir in olive oil, salt, and cooked vegetables.
5. Serve and enjoy.

Coconut Bread

(Total Time: 35 MIN | Serves: 6)

Ingredients:

¾ cup coconut flour

½ cup shredded coconut

2 tsp baking powder

½ tsp baking soda

½ tsp salt

6 eggs

3 tbsp. honey

½ cup coconut oil, melted

Directions:

1. Preheat air fryer to 360 degrees F.
2. In a bowl, combine the coconut flour, shredded coconut, baking powder, baking soda, and salt.
3. In a second bowl, combine the remaining ingredients until well mixed. Gradually add the wet mixture into the flour mixture. Mix until smooth and well combined.
4. Grease a bread pan which fits the fryer tray with oil. Bake for 35 minutes.
5. Serve and enjoy!

Cheesy Spaghetti

(Total Time: 20 MIN | Serves: 4)

Ingredients:

1 lb. dry spaghetti pasta

1 cup pre-made alfredo sauce

1 cup marinara sauce

½ cup shredded mozzarella cheese

½ cup ricotta cheese

1 tbsp. parsley, chopped

Directions:

1. Preheat the air fryer to 390 degrees F.
2. Bring a large pot of water to a boil and add the pasta. Cook for about 10 minutes or until the pasta is tender.
3. Drain the pasta and stir in the alfredo and marinara sauce. Stir just to coat the noodles in the sauce.
4. Place the pasta in the fryer tray (this may need to be done in batches). Drop the ricotta on top by the tbsp.. Sprinkle with mozzarella.
5. Bake for 10 minutes. Remove and sprinkle with parsley. Serve and enjoy!

Spinach Stuffed Cannelloni

(Total Time: 25 MIN | Serves: 4)

Ingredients:

9 cannelloni shells, cooked

3 cups tomato Sauce

2 cups alfredo sauce

2 tbsp. Parmesan cheese

1 egg

1 cup spinach, cooked

1 cup ricotta cheese

1 cup shredded mozzarella

Directions:

1. Preheat the fryer to 380 degrees F
2. Combine the spinach, ricotta, parmesan, garlic, and egg. Mix well.
3. Place the spinach mixture into a piping bag and fill the cannelloni shells. Place the filled shells on to the fryer try
4. Top with the alfredo and tomato sauce. Sprinkle mozzarella on top. Bake for 15 minutes.
5. Serve hot, enjoy!

Classic Dinner Rolls

(Total Time: 30 MIN | Serves: 12)

Ingredients:

2 tbsp. butter, melted

¼ cup warm water

½ cup warm milk

2 cups flour

2 tbsp. sugar

2 ¼ tsp active dry yeast

½ tsp. salt

Directions:

1. Preheat air fryer to 375 degrees F.
2. Combine the butter, water, and milk in a bowl. In a second bowl, combine the remaining ingredients and mix well. Gradually add the liquid ingredients to the flour. Mix until the dough is smooth.
3. Knead the dough until smooth and elastic. Then, cover the dough and let sit for 10 minutes.
4. Divide and shape the dough into 12 rolls. Place on an ungreased pan which will fit into the air fryer.
5. Bake for 20 minutes.
6. Enjoy!

Cheesy Stuffed Manicotti

(Total Time: 25 MIN | Serves: 4)

Ingredients:

8 Manicotti Shells, cooked

1 large egg

1 cups ricotta cheese

2 cups shredded mozzarella

1 cup grated Parmesan cheese

1 tbsp. dried parsley

3 cups alfredo sauce

Directions:

1. Preheat the air fryer to 350 degrees F.

2. Combine the egg, ricotta, one cup of the mozzarella, and parmesan cheese. Mix well. Place the filling into a piping bag and fill the manicotti shells with the mixture. Place the filled shells on the fryer tray.

3. Top with alfredo sauce and sprinkle the last cup of mozzarella on top. Bake for 15 minutes.

4. Remove and sprinkle parsley on top. Serve and enjoy!

Saffron Risotto

(Total Time: 35 MIN | Serves: 4)

Ingredients:

4 cups chicken broth

2 tbsp. butter, melted

½ cup yellow onion, minced

1 cup Arborio rice

2 cups dry wine

¼ cup of grated parmesan cheese

2 tbsp. fresh parsley, chopped

1 tsp saffron

Directions:

1. Combine the broth and saffron. Bring to a simmer.
2. Preheat the fryer to 320. Rinse the rice and place in the fryer. Drizzle the butter over top. Cook for 5 minutes. Remove from the fryer and add the onion. Cook for 5 more minutes.
3. Remove the rice and onion and place in a skillet on medium heat. Once hot, add the wine and cook until the wine is absorbed. Stir in 1 cup of the saffron brother and cook until it is absorbed. Repeat until all the broth is gone and rice is tender.
4. Stir in the parsley and parmesan. Serve and enjoy

Air Fried Cinnamon Biscuits

🕐   🍽

(Total Time: 10 MIN | Serves: 6)

Ingredients:

1 can premade buttermilk
   biscuits

2 tbsp. butter, melted

2 tbsp. cinnamon sugar

Directions:

1. Set the temperature to 375 degrees F
2. Place the biscuits on the fryer tray and brush with butter. Bake for 5 minutes, turn the biscuits and bake for 5 more minutes.
3. Top with cinnamon sugar. Serve hot.
4. Enjoy!

Asparagus and Parmesan Risotto

(Total Time: 30 MIN | Serves: 3)

Ingredients:

4 ½ cups vegetable broth, warm

1 tbsp. tomato paste

4 tbsp. butter, melted

2 cloves garlic, minced

½ cups onion, diced

2 cups Arborio rice

2⁄3 cup dry white wine

2 ½ cups fresh asparagus, cut into pieces of 1 inch each.

1 cup parmesan cheese

1 tsp salt

1 tsp ground black pepper

Directions:

1. Preheat hair fryer to 320 degrees. Rinse the rice and add to the air fryer. Cook for 5 minutes.
2. Remove and drizzle the butter over the top. Add the onion and garlic. Cook for 5 more minutes.
3. Remove and place the rice and onion in a hot pan. Stir in the tomato paste. Add the win and stir until the wine is absorbed. Add 1 cup of the broth, and cook until the broth is absorbed. Repeat until all the broth has been used.
4. Stir in the asparagus, salt, pepper, and parmesan.
5. Serve and enjoy!

Butternut Squash Risotto

(Total Time: 36 MIN | Serves: 4)

Ingredients:

2 cups butternut squash, diced small

3 tbsp. olive oil

1 tsp. salt

1 tsp. ground nutmeg

5 cups warm chicken broth

1 tsp fresh rosemary, chopped

1 tsp. fresh thyme, chopped

¼ cup yellow onion, diced

1 ¼ cups Arborio rice

½ cup dried cranberries, chopped

¼ cup grated parmesan cheese

Directions:

1. Preheat the air fryer to 390 degrees F.
2. Place the squash in the air fryer basket and drizzle with 1 tbsp. of the oil. Season with salt and nutmeg. Cook for 20 minutes.
3. In a skillet, heat the remaining oil. Add the onions, rosemary, and thyme, cook until onions are soft.
4. Add the Arborio rice and cook until the rice is lightly browned.
5. Add 1 cup of the broth, and stir until absorbed. Repeat until all the liquid is absorbed and rice is tender.
6. Stir in the cooked squash, cranberries, and parmesan.

Egg, Ham, and Cheese Biscuits

(Time: 35 Minutes \ Servings: 10)

Ingredients:

1½ cups flour

2 tsp. baking powder

1 tsp sugar

1 tsp salt

2 eggs

¼ cup milk

½ cup butter, cubed

1 cup deli ham, chopped

½ cup shredded cheddar cheese

Directions:

1. Preheat the air fryer to 390 degrees F.

2. Combine the flour, baking powder, sugar, salt, and butter. Press the ingredients together until the mixture is a fine crumb. Add the cheese and ham and mix well.

3. Create a well in the middle of the mixture. Place the eggs and milk into the well and mix until a stick dough forms.

4. Drop the mixture by the spoonful onto the baking tray. Bake for 20 minutes.

5. Serve warm and enjoy!

Mayo Broccoli and Cauliflower Egg Salad with Bacon

(Total Time: 20 MIN | Serves: 3-4)

Ingredients:

1 cup Mayonnaise

1 cup shredded Cheddar Cheese

1 cup Broccoli Florets

1 cup Cauliflower Florets

6 Bacon Slices

½ tbsp. Sugar

4 Eggs, diced

2 tbsp. Olive Oil

1 tbsp. Lemon Juice

Salt and Pepper, to taste

Directions:

1. Preheat your Air Fryer to 300 degrees F.
2. Add bacon, broccoli, and cauliflower.
3. Cook for 10 minutes.
4. Transfer the broccoli and cauliflower to a bowl and add the egg.
5. Crumble the bacon on top.
6. Whisk together the remaining ingredients, and season with some salt and pepper.
7. Toss to combine.
8. Serve and enjoy!

Roasted Pear and Roquefort Salad with Pecans

(Total Time: 20 MIN | Serves: 4)

Ingredients:

1 Avocado, peeled and diced

3 Pears, peeled and cored

½ cup sliced Onions

½ cup Pecan Halves

1 Lettuce, chopped

2 tbsp. White Sugar

Dressing:

¼ cup Olive Oil

1 tsp minced Garlic

3 tbsp. Red Wine Vinegar

Pinch of Lime Zest

1 ½ tsp Mustard

Pinch of Sea Salt

Directions:

1. Preheat your Air Fryer to 340 degrees F.
2. In a baking pan, combine the pecans and sugar.
3. Place the Air Fryer and cook for 5 minutes. Set aside
4. Add the pears in your Air Fryer, and cook for 5 minutes. Slice into thin slices.
5. In a bowl, combine the lettuce, pear, pecans, avocado, onions, and cheese.
6. In a small bowl, whisk together the dressing ingredients.
7. Pour the dressing over the salad.
8. Serve and enjoy!

Cranberry and Blue Cheese Roasted Carrot Salad

(Total Time: 30MIN | Serves: 4)

Ingredients:

¼ cup Slivered Almonds

3 ounces Blue Cheese

2 cups Arugula

½ cup Cranberries

1 ½ pounds Carrots, sliced

2 tbsp. Olive Oil

Dressing:

¼ cup Olive Oil

1 tbsp. Apple Cider Vinegar

1 tbsp. Honey

Pinch of Lemon Zest

Salt and Pepper, to taste

Directions:

1. Preheat your Air Fryer to 390 degrees F.
2. Add the carrots and almonds to the Air Fryer.
3. Drizzle with 2 tbsp. of oil over.
4. Air fry for 20 minutes.
5. Transfer to a bowl.
6. Add arugula, cranberries, and blue cheese.
7. Toss to combine.
8. Whisk together the dressing ingredients and pour the dressing over.
9. Serve and enjoy!

Cranberry, Almond, and Poppy Seed Cabbage Salad

(Total Time: 15 MIN | Serves: 4)

Ingredients:

½ cup Slivered Almonds

5 cups Shredded Cabbage

½ cup chopped Celery

½ cup diced Green Pepper

1 ½ cups dried Cranberries

1 cup of Mayonnaise

2 tbsp. minced Chives

1 tbsp. Poppy Seeds

2 tbsp. Mustard

1 tbsp. Honey

¼ tsp Salt

Pinch of Black Pepper

1 tbsp. Lemon Juice

Directions:

1. Preheat your Air Fryer to 340 degrees F.
2. Place the cranberries, cabbage, and almonds, in the air dryer.
3. Drizzle with olive oil and cook for 5 minutes.
4. Transfer to a bowl.
5. Add the green peppers, chives, and celery, and toss to combine.
6. In a small bowl, whisk together the rest of the ingredients.
7. Pour the mixture over the salad.
8. Toss to coat well.
9. Serve and enjoy!

Paprika Potato Wedges

(Total Time: 60 MIN | Serves: 4)

Ingredients:

1 tbsp. Paprika

3 Large Russet Potatoes

¼ tsp Garlic Powder

Salt and Pepper, to taste

1 tbsp. Olive Oil

Directions:

1. Fill a pot with water and bring to a boil over medium heat.
2. Add the potatoes and cook for 15 minutes.
3. Transfer to the freezer immediately, and let sit for 25 minutes.
4. Preheat your Air Fryer to 390 degrees F.
5. Cut the potatoes into wedges and place in the Air Fryer.
6. Sprinkle with salt, pepper, garlic powder and paprika.
7. Drizzle the oil over.
8. Cook for about 8 minutes. You may need to work in batches here, depending on the size of your Air Fryer.
9. Serve and enjoy!

Cheesy Potato Gratin

(Total Time: 30 MIN | Serves: 4)

Ingredients:

2 Eggs

1 tbsp. Flour

2 ounces Cheddar Cheese, grated

2 Eggs

3 Potatoes, sliced

½ cup Coconut Cream

1 tsp Olive Oil

Directions:

1. Preheat your Air Fryer to 380 degrees F.
2. Combine the potato slices with the oil in the Air Fryer.
3. Cook for 9 minutes.
4. Whisk together the eggs, coconut cream, and flour.
5. Grease a baking pan with some cooking spray.
6. Transfer the potatoes to the baking pan.
7. Pour the sauce over.
8. Sprinkle with cheese.
9. Air fry for 10 minutes.
10. Serve and enjoy!

Spicy Couscous with Peas and Chickpeas

(Total Time: 30 MIN | Serves: 4)

Ingredients:

½ cup Veggie Broth

1 cup grated Carrots

2 cups cooked Couscous

½ tsp Turmeric

½ tsp Hot Sauce

1 tsp Coriander

½ tsp Cardamom

¼ tsp Pepper

1 tsp Olive Oil

¼ tsp Salt

1 cup canned Chickpeas, drained

1 cup frozen Peas

1 tbsp. chopped Mint, for garnish

Directions:

1. Preheat your Air Fryer to 380 degrees F.
2. Add the peas, chickpeas, oil, and the spices in the Air Fryer.
3. Cook for 3 minutes, stirring once halfway through.
4. Stir in the rest of the ingredients.
5. Close the lid, lower the heat to 340 degrees F, and cook for 10 minutes.
6. Serve garnished with mint.
7. Enjoy!

Sherry Green Beans

(Total Time: 30 MIN | Serves: 4)

Ingredients:

2 tsp minced Garlic

1 tbsp. Olive Oil

1 pound Green Beans, trimmed

2 tbsp. Sherry

1 tsp Dark Sesame Oil

2 tbsp. chopped Green Onions

1 tbsp. toasted Sesame Seeds

Salt and Pepper, to taste

Directions:

1. Preheat your Air Fryer to 340 degrees F.
2. Combine the green beans and oil in your Air Fryer.
3. Cook for 10 minutes.
4. Add the remaining ingredients.
5. Season with some salt and pepper.
6. Stir to combine well.
7. Close the lid and air fry for 15 more minutes.
8. Serve and enjoy!

Baked Potatoes with Pepper and Onion

(Total Time: 60 MIN | Serves: 4)

Ingredients:

4 Medium Potatoes
1 Onion, finely chopped
1 Red Bell Pepper, diced
2 tbsp. Olive Oil
1 tsp Paprika
½ tsp Garlic Powder
¼ tsp Salt
Pinch o Pepper

Directions:

1. Place the potatoes in a bowl filled with water, and let soak for 25 minutes.
2. Preheat your Air Fryer to 380 degrees F.
3. Drain the potatoes and place in a bowl.
4. Add the remaining ingredients and toss to combine.
5. Transfer the potatoes to the Air Fryer. Make sure to top them with the onions and peppers.
6. Air Fry for 25-30 minutes.
7. Serve and enjoy!

French Fries

(Total Time: 25 MIN | Serves: 4)

Ingredients:

3 Large Potatoes
1 ½ tbsp. Coconut Oil
¼ tsp Garlic Powder
Salt to the taste

Directions:

1. Wash and skin potatoes, and then cut in sticks no more than ½ inch thick.
2. Place potato sticks in a bowl with water as you cut them.
3. Stir potato sticks by hand, drain the water and then fill the bowl again with water. Repeat this step two more times to wash all excess surface starch.
4. Drain potato sticks third time and then pat dry with a kitchen towel.
5. Transfer potato sticks in a bowl and add the coconut oil and garlic powder to them. Toss well to coat.
6. Transfer potatoes in the Air Fryer basket and cook for 15 minutes at 400 degrees F, shaking once or twice while cooking.
7. Season with salt and serve right away.
8. Enjoy!

Breaded Onion Rings

(Total Time: 12 MIN | Serves: 4)

Ingredients:

1 ¼ cup Plain Flour

½ tsp Salt

1 tsp Baking Powder

1 Egg

1 cup Milk

1 Large Onion, sliced and rings
    separated

1 cup Bread Crumbs

Directions:

1. Sift flour with salt and baking powder in a bowl, and then stir well with a fork to combine. Set aside.

2. Whisk egg in another bowl and then add milk and whisk together to combine. Set aside too.

3. Spread the breadcrumbs on larger plate and set aside.

4. Flour the onion rings, dip them in egg mixture and then dredge with the bread crumbs.

5. Place in the Air Fryer basket and cook for 10 minutes at 400 degrees F.

6. Serve while warm.

7. Enjoy!

Baked Potatoes

(Total Time: 45 MIN | Serves: 3)

Ingredients:

2 tbsp. Olive Oil

1 tsp Garlic, minced

1 tsp Parsley Leaves, chopped

1 tsp Salt

1 pinch Ground Black Pepper

3 Large Potatoes

3 tbsp. Sour Cream

1 tbsp. Grated Parmesan Cheese

1 tbsp. Chives, chopped

Directions:

1. Place the olive oil, garlic, salt, pepper and parsley leaves in a bowl and mix well to combine.
2. Wash well the potatoes and prick them with a fork roughly inch apart, all around.
3. Rub each potato with the oil and seasonings mix.
4. Place in the Air Fryer basket and cook for 40 minutes at 400 degrees F.
5. Just before the potatoes are baked mix together sour cream and parmesan.
6. Make an inch and half deep lengthwise cut on each potato and spread them a bit.
7. Spoon a third of the sour cream and parmesan mixture in the crevice and sprinkle with chopped chives.
8. Serve with a favorite style of steak.
9. Enjoy!

Roasted Mushrooms

(Total Time: 14 MIN | Serves: 4)

Ingredients:

1 tbsp. Herbs de Provence

1 tsp Ground Black Pepper

½ tsp Garlic Powder

½ tsp Salt

1 tbsp. Duck Fat or Olive Oil

2 lbs Button Mushrooms, quartered

2 tbsp. White Vermouth

Directions:

1. Preheat the Air Fryer to 400 degrees F for 3 minutes.
2. Place in the Air Fryer duck fat, herbs de Provence, pepper, salt, garlic and mushrooms. Toss to coat well.
3. Cook for 5 minutes.
4. Pour vermouth over mushrooms. Toss well, while being careful not to inhale too much of fumes, and cook for another 5 minutes at 400 degrees F.
5. Serve while still hot.
6. Enjoy!

Mashed Potato Cakes

(Total Time: 15-20 MIN | Serves: 4)

Ingredients:

1 cup Bread Crumbs

2 cups Mashed Potatoes

4 Eggs

1 cup Milk

1 cup Cheddar Cheese, grated

1 tsp Garlic Powder

1 tsp Dried Basil

2 cups Plain Flour

3 tsp Baking Powder

Salt to the taste

2 tbsp. Olive Oil

Directions:

1. Spread the breadcrumbs on a plate and set aside.
2. Place in a bowl all other ingredients, except the olive oil, and mix all well to combine.
3. Shape the mixture into eight 1 inch thick patties and then dredge them in bread crumbs.
4. Brush the bottom of Air Fryer accessory with the olive oil, and then place breaded patties in it.
5. Cook for 5 minutes at 400 degrees F.
6. Turn over the patties and drizzle with the rest of olive oil, and cook for another 5 minutes.
7. Serve warm.
8. Enjoy!

Roasted Brussels Sprouts

(Total Time: 16 MIN | Serves: 4)

Ingredients:

1 lbs Brussels Sprouts, halved

Salt to taste

Ground Black Pepper to taste

1 tbsp. Olive Oil

½ cup Mayonnaise

2 tbsp. Roasted Garlic, mashed

½ tsp Thyme, finely chopped

Directions:

1. Place the Brussels sprouts, olive oil, salt and pepper in bowl, and mix well to coat.

2. Transfer Brussels sprouts into Air Fryer accessory and cook for 15 minutes at 380 degrees F.

3. While Brussels sprouts are cooking combine the mayonnaise, garlic and thyme in a bowl and mix well.

4. Place roasted Brussels sprouts on plates and drizzle with the garlic mayonnaise.

5. Enjoy!

Air Fried Veggie Manchurian

(Total Time: 20 MIN | Serves: 4)

Ingredients:

2 Bell Peppers, steamed and chopped
4 ounces of Cabbage, steamed and chopped
1 cup cooked Rice
2 tbsp. Sesame Oil
4 tbsp. canned Beans
3 tbsp. Corn Flour
3 Garlic Cloves, minced
1 Onion, chopped
2 Carrots, steamed and chopped
4 tbsp. Soy Sauce
1 tbsp. Olive Oil
1 tsp Sugar
Salt and Pepper, to taste
2 tbsp. Chili Paste

Directions:

1. Preheat your Air Fryer to 390 degrees F.
2. Combine 2 tbsp. of the corn flour, carrots, peppers, rice, cabbage, and some salt and peppers.
3. Make balls out of this mixture, and place them in the Air Fryer.
4. Drizzle the olive oil over, close the lid, and cook for 8 minutes.
5. Transfer to a plate.
6. Whisk together the remaining ingredients in the Air Fryer and cook until the sauce thickens.
7. Pour the sauce over the balls.
8. Enjoy!

Air Fried Samousa

(Total Time: 30 MIN | Serves: 4)

Ingredients:

1 cup Peas, steamed

1 tbsp. Ajwain

1 tbsp. Aniseed

1/3 cup Water

1 tsp grated Ginger

2 cups Flour

2 Boiled Potatoes, cubed

4 tbsp. Olive Oil

1 tbsp. Coriander Seeds

1 tbsp. Chili Powder

1 tbsp. Cumin Seeds

1 tbsp. Masala

1 Green Chili, minced

Salt and Pepper, to taste

Directions:

1. Preheat your Air Fryer to 390 degrees F.
2. Combine 3 tbsp. of the oil, flour, ajwain, and some salt and pepper. The mixture should have the consistency of breadcrumbs.
3. Stir in the water, cover the bowl, and let sit for half an hour.
4. Heat 1 tsp of the oil in the Air Fryer.
5. Add the cumin seeds and cook until they start to pop.
6. Add ginger and chili and cook for 2 minutes.
7. Add masala and cook for 30 more seconds.
8. Transfer the mixture to a bowl.
9. Add the potatoes coriander seeds, chili powder, potato cubes, and peas. Stir to combine well.
10. Form balls out of the dough.
11. Cut them in half and shape the halves into cone-like shapes.
12. Divide the potato and pea filling between the cones.
13. Brush them with the remaining oil and arrange in the Air Fryer.
14. Air Fry for about 10 minutes.
15. Serve and enjoy!

Veggie and Cashew Rolls

(Total Time: 25 MIN | Serves: 4)

Ingredients:

6 Spring Roll Wrappers

1 tbsp. Olive Oil

2 Carrots, grated

1 small Zucchini, grated

1 Garlic Cloves, minced

A handful of Cashews, chopped

¼ tsp Ginger Powder

1 tbsp. Butter, melted

Directions:

1. Preheat your Air Fryer to 340 degrees F.
2. Place the oil, carrots, zucchini, garlic, and cashews in the Air Fryer.
3. Cook for 2 minutes.
4. Divide the mixture between the spring roll wrappers.
5. Wrap the rolls and brush with the melted butter.
6. Arrange in the Air Fryer.
7. Cook for 3 minutes.
8. Serve and enjoy!

Vegetarian Bean Patties

(Total Time: 20 MIN | Serves: 4)

Ingredients:

1 can Black Beans, drained

1 Egg

½ cup Breadcrumbs

½ Bell Pepper, chopped

½ Red Onion

2 Garlic Cloves

1 tbsp. Cumin

¼ tsp Salt

Pinch of Pepper

1 tbsp. Olive Oil

Directions:

1. Preheat your Air Fryer to 390 degrees F.
2. Place the veggies, egg, breadcrumbs, and spices, in the food processor.
3. Pulse until mashed.
4. Make 4 patties out of the mixture.
5. Place in the Air Fryer.
6. Drizzle the oil over.
7. Cook for 7 minutes.
8. Flip over and cook for additional 7 minutes.
9. Serve and enjoy!
10.

Snacks & Appetizers

Garlicky Zucchini Fries

(Total Time: 20 MIN | Serves: 3)

Ingredients:

¼ cup Cornstarch

1 ½ tsp Garlic Powder

4 Zucchinis

¼ cup Olive Oil

¼ cup Water

¼ tsp Salt

Pinch of Pepper

Directions:

1. Preheat your Air Fryer to 390 degrees F.
2. Cut the zucchini into ½-inch by 3-inch pieces.
3. Whisk together the cornstarch, oil, and water.
4. Line a baking dish with parchment paper.
5. Dip the zucchini in the batter, and then arrange on the prepared dish
6. Sprinkle with the spices.
7. Place in the Air Fryer and cook for 15 minutes.
8. Serve and enjoy!

Chips with Creamy and Cheesy Dip

(Total Time: 35 MIN | Serves: 3)

Ingredients:

2 Scallions, minced

3 tbsp. Olive Oil

¼ tsp Lemon Juice

1 cup Cream Cheese

½ cup Sour Cream

¼ tsp Garlic Powder

3 Large Russet Potatoes

Pinch of Sea Salt

Pinch of Pepper

Directions:

1. Preheat your Air Fryer to 300 degrees F.
2. Slice the potatoes thinly. Fill a bowl with water and soak them in it for about 10 minutes.
3. Pat dry with paper towels and place in the Air Fryer.
4. Drizzle with the oil and sprinkle with salt and pepper.
5. Air Fry for 20 minutes.
6. Meanwhile, whisk together the remaining ingredients.
7. Serve the chips with the dip.
8. Enjoy!

Lemony Roasted Bell Peppers

(Total Time: 10 MIN | Serves: 4)

Ingredients:

4 Bell Peppers

1 tsp Olive Oil

Pinch of Sea Salt

1 tbsp. Lemon Juice

1 tsp chopped Parsley

¼ tsp minced Garlic

Pinch of Pepper

Directions:

1. Preheat your Air Fryer to 390 degrees F.
2. Arrange the bell peppers in the Air Fryer and drizzle with the olive oil.
3. Air Fry for 5 minutes.
4. Transfer to a serving plate.
5. In a small bowl, combine the lemon juice, garlic, parsley, salt, and pepper.
6. Drizzle this mixture over the peppers.
7. Serve and enjoy!

Garlicky Eggplant Chips

(Total Time: 20 MIN | Serves: 2)

Ingredients:

1 Large Eggplant

½ cup Water

¼ cup Cornstarch

Pinch of Salt

¼ cup Olive Oil

1 tsp Garlic Powder

Directions:

1. Preheat your Air Fryer to 390 degrees F.
2. Peel and slice the eggplant thinly. Place the slice in a bowl.
3. Add the oil, water, and cornstarch to the bowl, and mix to combine well. Make sure that the eggplants are fully coated.
4. Transfer to the Air Fryer and sprinkle with salt and garlic powder.
5. Cook for 12 minutes.
6. Serve and enjoy!

Crunchy Onion Rings

(Total Time: 10 MIN | Serves: 2)

Ingredients:

¾ Cup Milk

1 Large Onion

1 cup Flour

1 tbsp. Baking Powder

1 Egg

¾ cup Breadcrumbs

¼ tsp Salt

¼ tsp Paprika

Directions:

1. Preheat your Air Fryer to 340 degrees F.
2. Whisk together the milk, eggs, flour, salt, and paprika in a bowl.
3. Peel and slice the onion. Separate into rings.
4. Grease the Air Fryer with some cooking spray.
5. Dip each onion ring into the batter and then coat with breadcrumbs.
6. Arrange in the Air Fryer.
7. Cook for 10 minutes.
8. Serve and enjoy!

Cheesy Slider

(Total Time: 15 MIN | Serves: 4)

Ingredients:

1 ½ pound ground beef

Salt and pepper to taste

8 dinner rolls, sliced in the middle

1 cup cheddar cheese, grated

Directions:

1. Season the beef with salt and pepper.
2. Take about 3 ounces of the beef, roll it in between your palms, and then flatten it out to patties.
3. Cook it in the fryer at 390°F for 10 minutes. Make sure to turn it over at 5-minute mark.
4. Once cooked, place the patty in the roll and top it with cheese.
5. If you want, you may put the rolls in the fryer once it is assembled then toast it for 30-60 seconds.

Onion-Cheese Puff Bites

(Total Time: 30 MIN | Serves: 8)

Ingredients:

7 ounces store-bough puff pastry

1 ½ ounces gouda cheese, shredded

1 green onion, sliced

2-3 tbsp. milk

Directions:

1. Divide the puff pastry into 16 equally sized squares.
2. Fill the center of each dough with cheese and onion, then fold it in triangle. Make sure to secure the edges.
3. Spread some milk all over the pastry.
4. Cook the pastry in the fryer at 390°F for 10 minutes.

Ham-Broccoli Quiche

(Total Time: 35 MIN | Serves: 8)

Ingredients:

3 ½ ounces pie crust dough,
   preferably a ready-made one

½ tbsp. vegetable oil

1 egg

1 ½ ounces cheddar cheese,
   grated

3 tbsp. whipping cream

1/8 tsp. pepper

1 ½ ounces broccoli florets,
   boiled and chopped into tiny
   pieces

1 ½ ounces ham, sliced into small
   pieces.

Directions:

1. Spread some oil in a pie mold.
2. Create 2 round pie dough with the size of your mold.
3. Take 1 dough and assemble it at the bottom of the well-greased mold. Set aside for a while.
4. In a bowl, whisk in the eggs until fluffy. Add the cheese and cream. Season it with salt and pepper.
5. Assemble the ham and broccoli on the pie dough. Pour in the egg mixture.
6. Top the mold with the other round dough. Make sure to seal the edges.
7. Cook it in the preheated air fryer at 390°F for 10-12 minutes.

Mexican Empanada

(Total Time: 40 MIN | Serves: 20)

Ingredients:

1 shallot, chopped

¼ red bell pepper, diced

4 ½ ounces chorizo, cubed

2 tbsp. parsley

7 ounces store-bought pizza
   dough

Directions:

1. In a pan over medium heat, sauté the pepper, shallots, and chorizo together for 3-5 minutes. Turn the heat off before adding in the parsley.

2. Take 20 small rounds from the dough. You may use a cookie cutter if you want.

3. Scoop out some of the chorizo mixture and place it on the center of each round of dough. Fold and secure the edges. Do the same for the rest of the ingredients.

4. Cook the empanadas in the air fryer at 390°F for 10-12 minutes.

Homemade Sunflower Bread

(Total Time: 90 MIN | Serves: 4)

Ingredients:
3 ½ ounces whole wheat flour
3 ½ ounces all-purpose flour
1 tsp salt
1 tsp instant yeast
1 ½ ounces sunflower seeds
200 ml water

Directions:
1. Sift all the dry ingredients together in a large mixing bowl.
2. Gradually pour in the water while continuously stirring.
3. Flour your counter top. This will prevent the dough from sticking while you knead it.
4. Once all the ingredients are incorporated, take the dough out of the bowl and put it on the floured countertop.
5. Knead the dough until smooth. Roll it into a bowl. Top it with cling film and let it rise for half an hour.
6. Once risen, brush the top with water.
7. Transfer the dough in a cake dish. Place it in a preheated air fryer at 390°F and cook for 18-20 minutes.

Mushroom–Salami Pizza

(Total Time: 30 MIN | Serves: 2)

Ingredients:

1 tsp butter, melted

¼ cup tomato sauce

1 small, store-bought 8-in pizza dough

½ ball of mozzarella, sliced thinly

½ tbsp. olive oil

3 mushrooms, sliced

1 ½ ounces salami, cut into strips

Pepper to taste

2 tsp dried oregano

2 tbsp. Parmesan cheese, grated

Directions:

1. Press and pat the dough on a well-greased pizza pan. Use the butter to grease the pan.
2. Spread the sauce all over the dough then top it all with cheese.
3. Now, sprinkle the mushrooms and salami over the pizza base. Season it with oregano, pepper, and cheese.
4. Cook it in a preheated air-fryer at 390°F for 12 minutes.

Breaded Calamari with Salsa Dip

(Total Time: 20 MIN | Serves: 2)

Ingredients:

1 ½ pounds squid, sliced into
    rings

¼ tsp. salt

1/8 tsp. black pepper

1 cup all-purpose flour

2 eggs, whisked

1 cup breadcrumbs

½ cup salsa

Directions:

1. Set the air fryer to 365°F.
2. Season the calamari with salt and pepper. You may add any other herbs and spices you want.
3. Coat it with a generous amount of flour, then dip it into the eggs, then coat with bread crumbs.
4. Cook it in the air fryer for 10-12 minutes.

Thai-Inspired Vegan Spring Rolls

(Total Time: 40 MIN | Serves: 8)

Ingredients:

2 onions, chopped

8 cloves garlic, minced

1 carrot, julienne cut

2 cups cabbage, shredded

1 tsp soy sauce

1 tbsp. pepper

1 tsp sugar

½ tsp salt

2 tbsp. vegetable oil

2 tbsp. corn flour

1 tsp water

10 spring roll sheets

Directions:

1. In an oiled pan over medium high heat, sauté the garlic and onion for 5 minutes or until the onion caramelizes.

2. Add the cabbage and carrots. Season it with salt, pepper, soy sauce, and a little bit of sugar. Cook for another 3-5 minutes then turn the heat of and set aside for a while.

3. Mix the water and corn flour in a shallow bowl. This will serve at the 'paste' for the spring rolls.

4. Lay out 1 spring roll on your countertop. Put some veggies in the middle. Fold the spring roll, then roll and secure the edges with the corn flour paste. Do the same for the rest of the ingredients.

5. Put the rolls in a preheated air fryer at 350°F and cook it for 20 minutes. Make sure you flip it on the other side at the 10 minute mark so it will be cooked evenly.

Fish Croquettes

(Total Time: 30 MIN | Serves: 6-8)

Ingredients:

15 ounces salmon flakes, mashed

1 cup parsley, chopped

2 eggs, beaten

1/8 tsp. black pepper

3 ½ ounces breadcrumbs

⅓ cup vegetable oil

Directions:

1. In a small bowl, mix the oil and crumbs. Set aside for a while.
2. Mix the salmon, eggs, parsley, and pepper in a bowl.
3. Scoop about 1-2 tbsp. of the mixture and roll into a ball.
4. Coat the balls with the crumb mixture.
5. Cook the balls in a preheated air fryer at 390°F for 7-10 minutes.

Mushroom Roast

(Total Time: 15 MIN | Serves: 4)

Ingredients:

2 pounds mushrooms, sliced

1 tbsp. butter

½ tsp garlic powder

1 tsp dried rosemary

1 tsp dried basil

Directions:

1. Mix everything in a large bowl. You may want to marinate it for about half an hour.
2. Preheat the air fryer at 320°F.
3. When the mushrooms are ready, just put it in the fryer and cook for 12-15 minutes. Stir it every 4-5 minutes to make sure it is evenly cooking.

Poked Potatoes

(Total Time: 190 MIN | Serves: 4-6)

Ingredients:

3 potatoes

1 tbsp. olive oil

¼ tbsp. salt

½ tbsp. garlic powder

1 tsp parsley

1 cup sour cream, garnish

Directions:

1. In a small bowl, mix the salt, parsley, and garlic powder together.
2. Pierce the potatoes all over with a fork.
3. Drizzle it with some oil, and then rub in the spice-herb mix you made earlier.
4. Cook the potatoes in a preheated air fryer at 390°F for 30-35 minutes.

Crispy Potato Wedges with Paprika

(Total Time: 90 MIN | Serves: 6)

Ingredients:

6 potatoes, cut into wedges and
   boiled al dente

2 tbsp. olive oil

1 ½ tsp paprika

¼ tsp. salt

1/8 tsp. black pepper

Directions:

1. Preheat the air fryer at 390°F.
2. Mix the paprika, salt, pepper, and olive oil in a small bowl.
3. Roll the potato wedges on the paprika mix.
4. Cook the spiced wedges in the air fryer for 15 minutes or until crispy.

Classic French Fries

(Total Time: 90 MIN | Serves: 8)

Ingredients:

6 potatoes, peeled and slice into
   sticks

1 bowl cold water

2 tbsp. olive oil

Directions:

1. Immerse the potato sticks in a bowl of cold water for 30-45 minutes. This will reduce its starch content, hence, make the fries crispier.

2. After half an hour, drain the cold water and pat the sticks dry.

3. Drench it in olive oil and cook in the preheated air fryer at 360°F for 30 minutes. Make sure to stir it every 10 minutes to make sure it is evenly cooked.

Meatballs with Mexican Sauce

(Total Time: 45 MIN | Serves: 6)

Ingredients:

12 ounces ground beef

½ tbsp. fresh thyme leaves, chopped

1 tbsp. fresh parsley, chopped

1 onion, chopped

3 tbsp. breadcrumbs

1 egg, whisked

¼ tsp. salt

1/8 tsp. black pepper

10 ounces marinara sauce

Directions:

1. In a large bowl, mix the beef, thyme, parsley, crumbs, onions, and eggs together. Season everything with salt and pepper.

2. Scoop a bit of the mixture and form it into a ball in between your palms.

3. Cook it in the air fryer at 390°F for 8-10 minutes.

4. Pour in the marinara and cook for another 5-7 minutes.

Fried Shrimps in Bacon Blanket

(Total Time: 30 MIN | Serves: 4)

Ingredients:

16 pieces shrimp, peeled and
   deveined

16 slices bacon

1 cup sour cream, dip

Directions:

1. Preheat the air fryer at 390°F.
2. Wrap the shrimps with bacon.
3. Place it in the fryer, in batches, and cook for 5-7 minutes.
4. Serve with a cup of sour cream as dip.

Cheesy Croquettes

(Total Time: 65 MIN | Serves: 4)

Ingredients:

1 block cheddar cheese

1 pound bacon

4 tbsp. olive oil

1 cup breadcrumbs

1 cup all-purpose flour

2 eggs, whisked

Directions:

1. Mix the crumbs and oil together. Set aside for a while.
2. Slice the cheese into 6 equally-proportioned sticks. Wrap each stick with 2 bacon strips. Dip it in the eggs.
3. Coat each wrapped stick with the crumbs.
4. Air fry the bacon-cheese sticks at 390°F for 10 minutes or until the bacon is crispy on the outside.

Feta Bites

(Total Time: 60 MIN | Serves: 4)

Ingredients:

1 egg yolk, whisked

4 ounces feta cheese

1 scallion, chopped

2 tbsp. parsley, chopped

Black pepper to taste

2 tbsp. olive oil

2 sheets frozen filo pastry, thawed

Directions:

1. Slice the filo into squares. Set aside for a while.

2. In a bowl, mix the eggs, cheese, parsley, salt, pepper, and scallion together.

3. Fill each filo squares with the cheese mixture. Fold the filo to a triangle and secure the edges.

4. Cook it in the air fryer at 360°F for 5-7 minutes.

Korean Style Chicken BBQ

(Total Time: 90 MIN | Serves: 4)

Ingredients:

12 ounces boneless and skinless chicken breast, sliced into strips

½ cup pineapple juice

½ cup low sodium soy sauce

¼ cup sesame oil

4 scallions, chopped

4 cloves garlic, chopped

2 tsp sesame seeds, toasted

1 tbsp. fresh ginger, grated

¼ tsp. black pepper

Directions:

1. Mix the following together in a large bowl: soy sauce, pineapple juice, oil, garlic, scallions, ginger, sesame seeds, and pepper.

2. Soak the chicken into the soy sauce mix and let it marinate for at least an hour.

3. After 1 hour, skew the chicken. Cook it in the air fryer at 390°F for 7-10 minutes.

Meatballs with Yogurt Dip

(Total Time: 40 MIN | Serves: 4)

Ingredients:

MEATBALLs
¼ cup olive oil
4 ounces ground turkey
1 pound ground lamb
1 tbsp. mint, chopped
1 ½ tbsp. parsley, chopped
1 tsp ground coriander
1 tsp cayenne pepper
1 tsp ground cumin
1 tsp red chili paste
1 egg white
2 cloves garlic, minced
1 tsp salt

DIP:
½ cup nonfat Greek yogurt
¼ cup sour cream
2 tbsp. buttermilk
¼ cup mint, chopped
1 clove garlic, minced
Salt to taste

Directions:

1. In a large bowl, mix together all the ingredients for the meatballs.
2. Take 1-2 tbsp. of the mixture and roll it into a ball. Do the same for the rest of the mixture.
3. Cook the meatballs in the air fryer at 390°F for 8-10 minutes.
4. Meanwhile, for the dip, whisk in the yogurt, sour cream, buttermilk, mint, and garlic together. Season it with some salt.
5. Once the meatballs are cooked, transfer it to a serving plate together with the creamy yogurt dip.

Air Fried Pigs in a Blanket

(Total Time: 30 MIN | Serves: 4)

Ingredients:

1 package cocktail franks

8 ounces crescent rolls

Directions:

1. Roll out the crescent dough and slice it into strips.
2. Wrap the strips all over the cocktail franks and secure it with a toothpick. Let it rest in the fridge for 5 minutes.
3. While the pigs are resting, preheat the air fryer to 330°F.
4. Cook the franks in the fryer for 7 minutes.
5. Crank up the temperature to 390°F and cook the pigs further for 2-3 minutes.

Stuffed Portobello

(Total Time: 90 MIN | Serves: 4)

Ingredients:

8 Portobello mushrooms
1 slice white bread, ground
1 clove garlic, minced
1 tbsp. parsley, chopped
1/8 tsp. black pepper
1 tbsp. olive oil

Directions:

1. Process the bread in a food processor until it turns to powder-like texture.
2. Toss in the parsley, garlic, and pepper into the blender and pulse to blend.
3. Gradually pour in the oil while pulsing.
4. Evenly divide the mixture into the mushrooms.
5. Cook the mushrooms in the air fryer at 390°F for 8-10 minutes.

Mini Calzone

(Total Time: 30 MIN | Serves: 4)

Ingredients:

Dough:

1 tsp Yeast

3 tbsp. Sugar

4 cups Flour

1 ½ cups Water

Pinch of Salt

Filling:

1 tbsp. Olive Oil

1 ½ tbsp. Tomato Puree

2 Tomatoes, diced

3 Garlic Cloves, minced

1 tbsp. Chili Powder

1 tbsp. chopped Parsley

3 tbsp. diced Bell Pepper

¼ tsp Onion Powder

1 tsp Oregano

1 tsp Thyme

4 tbsp. grated Cheddar Cheese

Directions:

1. Preheat your Air Fryer to 390 degrees F.
2. Combine the dough ingredients in a bowl, cover it, and set aside.
3. Heat the oil in your Air Fryer.
4. Add garlic, onion powder, oregano, thyme, and bell pepper, and cook for 1 minute.
5. Add tomatoes and tomato puree, and cook for 3 more minutes.
6. Stir in the chili powder and cheeses and cook for 1 more minute.
7. Divide the dough into 4 equal pieces.
8. Spoon the filling onto the dough pieces.
9. Close the dough and seal the edges with a fork.
10. Prick the top of the calzone with a toothpick in a couple of places.
11. Line the Air Fryer with a piece of parchment paper and arrange the mini calzone in it.
12. Cook for 7 minutes.
13. Serve and enjoy!

Air Fried Corn Dogs

(Total Time: 45 MIN | Serves: 8)

Ingredients:

1 cup Oatmeal

1 Egg

1 cup of Milk

¼ cup Sugar

1 cup Flour

16 Hot Dogs

4 tsp Baking Powder

½ cup Oil

Salt and Pepper, to taste

Directions:

1. Combine the flour, cornmeal, sugar, and baking powder, in a bowl. Season with some salt and pepper.
2. Add the milk and egg and stir until the mixture becomes smooth.
3. Refrigerate for 5 minutes.
4. Meanwhile, preheat your Air Fryer to 350 degrees F.
5. Working in batches, cook the hot dogs in your Air Fryer for 5 minutes.
6. Place a piece of parchment paper in the Air Fryer.
7. Dip the cooked hot dogs in the batter and arrange them in the Air Fryer. Again, you will have to work in two batches.
8. Cook for 4 minutes.
9. Serve and enjoy!
10.

Desserts

Chocolate Brandy Cake

(Total Time: 35 MIN | Serves: 8)

Ingredients:

1 egg

½ cup milk

¼ cup vegetable oil

1 tsp vanilla extract

½ cup brandy

1/3 cup brown sugar

½ cup flour

¼ cup cocoa powder

¾ tsp. baking soda

¾ tsp. baking powder

½ tsp salt

Directions:

1. Preheat the fryer to 320 degrees F.

2. In a large bowl, combine the egg, milk, vanilla, and brandy. Stir until combined.

3. In a second bowl, combine the remaining ingredients. Gradually add the liquid ingredients to the flour mixture and stir just until combined. The batter should be thing.

4. Spray a cake pan, which fits into the air fryer basket, with nonstick spray. Pour the batter into the pan. Cover with foil. Poke a few holes in to the foil top and bake for 30 minutes.

5. Remove the foil and bake for 5 more minutes. Remove from the air frying and cool completely before serving.

6. Enjoy!

Chocolate Cherry Tart

(Total Time: 40 MIN | Serves: 8)

Ingredients:

1 cup dark chocolate, melted

2 tbsp. sugar

1 tsp. almond extract

¼ cup flour

1 cup cherries, pit removed and
cut in half

1 tube premade sugar cookie
dough

Directions:

1. Preheat air fryer to 325 degrees F.
2. Press the sugar cooking dough into a tart pan. Bake for 10 minutes.
3. In a bowl, combine the cherries, almond extract, flour, and sugar.
4. Pour the chocolate into the bottom of the baked cookie shell. Top with cherry mixture.
5. Bake for 30 minutes.
6. Cool completely before serving.
7. Enjoy!

Apple Pie

(Total Time: 45 MIN | Serves: 6)

Ingredients:

2 cups dried apples

6 oz. pre-made pie dough

1 tbsp. butter, melted

1 tsp. ground cinnamon

½ cup of sugar

2 tbsp. water

Directions:

1. Preheat the air fryer to 325 degrees F.
2. Combine all ingredients except for the pie dough in a small pot. Bring the mixture to a simmer and mix well. Simmer, stirring constantly, for one minute and remove the mixture for the oven.
3. Roll the dough to ¼ inch thick. Carefully place on to the fryer tray. Spoon the apples into the center, leaving about 1 inch on each side of the dough.
4. Fold over the extra inch on the dough sides over the apples. It's ok if some of the apples show in the middle.
5. Cook for 30 minutes or until browned.
6. Serve and enjoy!

Air Fried Chocolate Cake

(Total Time: 35 MIN | Serves: 4)

Ingredients:

1 egg

½ cup milk

¼ cup vegetable oil

1 tsp vanilla extract

½ cup hot coffee

1/3 cup brown sugar

½ cup flour

¼ cup cocoa powder

¾ tsp. baking soda

¾ tsp. baking powder

½ tsp salt

Directions:

1. Preheat the fryer to 320 degrees F.
2. In a large bowl, combine the egg, milk, vanilla, and coffee. Stir until combined.
3. In a second bowl, combine the remaining ingredients. Gradually add the liquid ingredients to the flour mixture and stir just until combined. The batter should be thing.
4. Spray a cake pan, which fits into the air fryer basket, with nonstick spray. Pour the batter into the pan. Cover with foil. Poke a few holes in to the foil top and bake for 30 minutes.
5. Remove the foil and bake for 5 more minutes. Remove from the air frying and cool completely before serving.
6. Enjoy!

Chocolate Caramel Peanut Cake

(Total Time: 20 MIN | Serves: 8)

Ingredients:

1 Box chocolate cake mix

3 eggs

½ cup oil

½ cup water

1 cup caramel sauce

1 cup heavy cream

1 tbsp. powdered sugar

1 cup chocolate syrup

½ cup chopped peanuts

Directions:

1. Preheat the air fryer to 320 degrees F
2. Mix together the cake mix, egg, oil, and water. Place in a cake pan that fits in the air fryer and bake for 20 minutes.
3. Remove the cake from the fryer. Spread the caramel sauce on top while still hot. Refrigerate until cold.
4. Meanwhile, combine the heavy cream and powdered sugar on high speed in a mixing bowl. Whip until fluffy. Spread over cooled cake. Sprinkle peanuts on top
5. Serve and enjoy!

Cinnamon Doughnuts

(Total Time: 20 MIN | Serves: 10)

Ingredients:

½ cup sugar

2¼ cups cake flour

1½ tsp baking powder

2 tbsp. butter, cold

1 tsp salt

2 beaten egg yolks

1 egg white

½ cup sour cream

½ cup vegetable oil

1 cup sugar

2 tsp. cinnamon

Directions:

1. Preheat fryer to 320 degrees F.
2. In a bowl, combine the sugar and butter. Stir until the mixture is crumbly. Add the egg yolks and whites. stir until smooth.
3. In another bowl, add the flour, the baking powder and the salt.
4. Add half the flour and half the sour cream mixture to the sugar mixture. Stir well then add remaining flour and sour cream. Refrigerate for 1 hour.
5. On a lightly floured surface, roll the dough ½ inch thick and cut into small circles.
6. Brush with the oil and set in the fryer basket. Cook for 10 minutes. Sprinkle with cinnamon while still hot.
7. Serve and enjoy.

Chocolate Orange Fudge Cake

(Total Time: 25 MIN | Serves: 4)

Ingredients:

2 tbsp. self rising flour

4 tbsp. sugar

2 cups dark chocolate, melted

2 cups butter, melted

1 tbsp. orange zest

1 tbsp. orange juice

2 large eggs

Directions:

1. Preheat the air fryer to 320 degrees F. Spray a cake pan which fits in the air fryer with not stick spray.

2. Combine the chocolate and butter, whisk until smooth.

3. In a second bowl, combine the sugar and egg. Whisk well.

4. Add the sugar mixture, orange zest, and orange juice in to the chocolate mixture. Add the flour and mix well.

5. Pour into the cake pan. Bake for 20 minutes.

6. Remove cake from the fryer and flip upside down. Tap the pan and remove the cake from the pan.

7. Serve and enjoy!

Peanut Butter Chocolate Poke Cake

(Total Time: 25 MIN | Serves: 12)

Ingredients:

1 Box chocolate cake mix

½ cup Vegetable oil

3 Eggs

½ cup water

1 cup chocolate syrup

1 cup creamy peanut butter

2 cups whipped cream

Directions:

1. Preheat the air fryer to 325 degrees. Spray a cake pan that fits the air fryer with not stick spray

2. Combine the cake mix, oil, eggs, and water. Mix well. Pour into the prepared cake pan and cook for 20 minutes or until a tooth pick inserted into the center comes out clean. Cool completely.

3. Poke 10 – 20 holes into the cake. Pour the chocolate syrup over the cake and let absorb.

4. Combine the peanut butter and whipped cream and mix well. Coat the entire cake with the mixture. Refrigerate before serving.

5. Enjoy.

Chocolate Peanut Butter Cake

(Total Time: 25 MIN | Serves: 12)

Ingredients:

1 egg

¾ cup milk

¼ cup vegetable oil

1 tsp vanilla extract

½ cup creamy peanut butter

½ cup chopped peanuts

1/3 cup brown sugar

½ cup flour

¼ cup cocoa powder

¾ tsp. baking soda

¾ tsp. baking powder

½ tsp salt

Directions:

1. Preheat the fryer to 320 degrees F.
2. In a large bowl, combine the egg, milk, vanilla, and peanut butter. Stir until combined.
3. In a second bowl, combine the remaining ingredients. Gradually add the liquid ingredients to the flour mixture and stir just until combined. The batter should be thin. Stir in the peanuts
4. Spray a cake pan, which fits into the air fryer basket, with nonstick spray. Pour the batter into the pan. Cover with foil. Poke a few holes in to the foil top and bake for 30 minutes.
5. Remove the foil and bake for 5 more minutes. Remove from the air frying and cool completely before serving.
6. Enjoy!

Triple Chocolate Cheese cake

(Total Time: 25 MIN | Serves: 6)

Ingredients:

2 cups crushed Oreo cookies

3 tbsp. of melted butter

1 cup cream cheese

½ cup sugar

3 eggs

½ cup of sour cream

½ cup heavy cream

½ cup cream de cacao liqueur

¼ cup flour

1 tsp vanilla extract

1 cup semi sweet chocolate chips

¼ cup cocoa powder

Directions:

1. Preheat the air fryer to 320 degrees F.
2. Combine the Oreos and butter until well combined.
3. Spray a springform pan which will fit into the air fryer basket with non stick spray. Press the Oreo mixture into the pan.
4. Whip together the cream cheese, sugar, liqueur, chocolate chips, flour, cocoa, vanilla, sour cream, and egg until smooth. Pour over the crust into an even layer.
5. Bake for 30 minutes, or until a tooth pick inserted into the center of the cake comes out clean.
6. Cool completely, enjoy!

Air Fried Banana Cake

(Total Time: 35 MIN | Serves: 4)

Ingredients:

2 tbsp. butter, melted

1 egg

1 medium ripe banana, mashed

2 tbsp. honey

½ cup brown sugar

1 cup flour

½ tsp. baking soda

½ tsp. baking powder

¼ tsp. salt

½ tsp. cinnamon

Directions:

1. Preheat the air fryer to 320 degrees F.
2. In a large bowl, combine the butter, egg, banana, and honey. Mix until well combined. Stir in the remaining ingredients just until combined.
3. Spray a cake pan which will fit into the air fryer basket with non stick spray. Pour the batter in to the pan.
4. Bake for 30 minutes, or until a tooth pick inserted into the center of the cake comes out clean.
5. Enjoy!

Chocolate Chiffon Cake

(Total Time: 35 MIN | Serves: 10)

Ingredients:

3 egg yolks

½ cup sugar

½ cup milk

½ cup vegetable oil

¼ cup cake flour

½ tsp baking powder

¼ cup cocoa powder

4 egg whites

⅓ tsp cream of tartar

Directions:

1. Preheat the air fryer to 320 degrees F.
2. Mix the yolks egg yolks and half the sugar in a small bowl.
3. In a second bowl combine the milk and olive oil. Mix well. Add in the flour, baking powder, and cocoa powder.
4. Add the yolk mixture to the flour mixture. Mix well until very smooth.
5. In a large mixing bowl, combine the egg whites and cream of tarter. Mix on high until soft peaks form. Add remaining sugar and mix on high speed until stiff peaks form.
6. Gradually add the egg white mixture to the cake batter and carefully stir. Pour in to a cake pan.
7. Bake for 20 minutes or until a toothpick inserted into the center comes out clean. Cool completely before slicing.
8. Serve and enjoy!

Scones

(Total Time: 15 MIN | Serves: 12)

Ingredients:

2 cups flour

4 tbsp. baking powder

2 tbsp. sugar

1 pinch salt

4 tbsp. butter

1 cup buttermilk

1 cup raisins, chopped

Directions:

1. Preheat the air fryer to 390 degrees F.
2. In a large bowl, combine the flour, baking powder, sugar, and salt. Mix well. Add the butter and press the mixture together until crumble. Create a well in the center and add the buttermilk and raisins. Mix until just combined and the mixture is sticky.
3. Drop by the spoon fool on to a baking sheet spray with nonstick spray. Bake for 15 minutes or until golden brown.
4. Serve warm and enjoy!

Chocolate Espresso Cake

🕐   🍽️

(Total Time: 20 MIN | Serves: 6)

Ingredients:

¼ cup butter

½ cup sugar

1 cup semi-sweet chocolate chips, melted

½ cup flour

1 tbsp. instant espresso powder

¼ tsp salt

3 large eggs

1 tsp vanilla

Directions:

1. Preheat the air fryer to 400 degrees F. Spray a muffin tin with non stick spray.

2. Mix the butter and sugar until fluffy. Add the eggs, one at a time, and mix until well combined.

3. Add remaining ingredients and mix until smooth.

4. Fill the muffin cups half way and bake for 15 minutes.

5. Serve hot and enjoy!

Dark Chocolate Truffles

(Total Time: 15 MIN | Serves: 10)

Ingredients:

3 cups dark chocolate chips,
   melted
¼ cup coconut oil
3 tbsp. orange juice
1 tsp vanilla extract
½ cup honey
1 tbsp. heavy cream
2 tbsp. flour
¼ cup cocoa powder

Directions:

1. Preheat fryer to 240 degrees.
2. Combine all ingredients except cocoa powder until smooth. Mixture will be thick.
3. Roll into balls and roll into the cocoa powder.
4. Bake for 10 minutes.
5. Cool, serve, and enjoy!

Strawberry Butter Cake

(Total Time: 35 MIN | Serves: 8)

Ingredients:

1 cup butter

1 cup sugar

1 tsp vanilla extract

6 egg yolks

2¾ cups flour

¼ tsp salt

¼ cup strawberry jam

Directions:

1. Preheat the air fryer to 350 degrees. Spray a cake pan with nonstick spray.
2. Mix butter and sugar until fluffy. Add the vanilla and egg yolks one at a time. Mix well.
3. Gradually add the flour and salt. Mix just until combined. Pour into cake pan and bake for 20 minutes.
4. Spread jam on top while still hot.
5. Cool, serve and enjoy!

Rum Cake

(Total Time: 35 MIN | Serves: 8)

Ingredients:

1 cup walnuts, chopped

1 package yellow cake mix

1 package vanilla pudding mix

4 large eggs

½ cup water

½ cup vegetable oil

½ cup dark rum

Directions:

1. Preheat the air fryer to 330 degrees F. Spray a cake pan that will fit into the air fryer with non-stick spray.
2. Combine all ingredients and mix well. Pour into prepared cake pan.
3. Bake for 30 minutes.
4. Cool completely before serving.
5. Enjoy!

Date Nut Loaf

(Total Time: 40 MIN | Serves: 7)

Ingredients:

3 large eggs

2 tbsp. coconut oil, melted

2 tbsp. coconut milk

3 tbsp. honey

½ tsp vanilla extract

¼ cup coconut flour

½ tsp baking powder

¼ tsp salt

½ cup dates, chopped

½ cup walnuts, chopped

Directions:

1. Preheat the air fryer to 350 degrees F.
2. In a large bowl, combine the eggs, coconut oil, coconut milk, honey, and vanilla. Mix well.
3. Add the flour, baking powder, and salt. Mix until no lumps remain. Fold in the dates and walnuts.
4. Form into a loaf and place on the fryer baking tray. Bake for 30 minutes.
5. Cool before serving.
6. Enjoy!

Carrot Raisin Bread

(Total Time: 45 MIN | Serves: 7)

Ingredients:

6 large eggs

¼ cup coconut oil, melted

3 tbsp. coconut milk

½ cup of honey

½ tsp almond extract

½ cup coconut flour

1 tsp baking powder

1 tsp baking soda

1 cup finely shredded carrots

½ cup walnuts, chopped

½ cup raisins, chopped

1 tsp ground cinnamon

½ tsp ground ginger

½ tsp ground clove

½ tsp salt

Directions:

1. Preheat the air fryer to 340 degrees F.
2. In a large sized bowl, combine the eggs, coconut oil, coconut milk, almond extract, salt, and honey.
3. Add the remaining ingredients except for the carrots, walnuts, and raisings. Mix well until the mixture is smooth.
4. Fold in the carrots, the walnuts and the raisins.
5. Spray a bread pan with nonstick spray and place the batter into the pan. Bake for 40 minutes.
6. Let cool before serving.
7. Enjoy!

Chocolate Zucchini Bread

🕐   🍽️

(Total Time: 50 MIN | Serves: 6)

Ingredients:

2 oz unsweetened chocolate, melted

3 large eggs

2 cups sugar

1 cup vegetable oil

2 cups grated zucchini

1 tsp vanilla extract

2 cups flour

1 tsp baking soda

1 tsp salt

1 tsp ground cinnamon

¾ cup semisweet chocolate chips

Directions:

1. Preheat the air fryer to around 350 degrees F. Spray two bread pans with nonstick spray and set aside.

2. In a large bowl, combine the eggs, sugar, oil, grated zucchini, vanilla, and the chocolate. Mix well. Add the remaining ingredient and mix until smooth. Pour batter into the prepared bread pans.

3. Bake for 40 minutes.

4. Cool completely before serving.

5. Enjoy!

Chocolate Biscuits

(Total Time: 30 MIN | Serves: 5)

Ingredients:

2 cups flour

½ cup sugar

1 egg

½ tsp salt

2 tbsp. cocoa powder

½ cup butter, cubed

¼ cup milk

Directions:

1. Preheat air fryer to 350 degrees.
2. Combine the flour sugar, salt, cocoa, and butter. Press together to form pea sized crumbs.
3. Create a well in the center of the mixture and add the egg and milk. Mix well until combined and dough is sticky.
4. Drop by the spoonful onto the fryer tray. Cook for 20 minutes.
5. Serve warm.
6. Enjoy!

Banana Walnut Bread

⏱ 🍽

(Total Time: 45 MIN | Serves: 7)

Ingredients:

2 ½ cups flour

1 tsp baking powder

½ tsp baking soda

½ tsp salt

1 cup sugar

½ cup butter, softened

2 tbsp. milk

2 medium ripe bananas, mashed

½ cup walnuts, chopped

Directions:

1. Preheat air fryer to 350 degrees F.

2. In a bowl, combine the butter, sugar, egg, and banana. Mix well. Stir in the remaining ingredients, just until combined.

3. Pour the batter into a bread pan which fits into the air fryer.

4. Cook for 45 minutes or until a tooth pick inserted into the center comes out clean.

5. Enjoy!

Palmier Biscuits

(Total Time: 15 MIN | Serves: 8)

Ingredients:

1 lb. pre-made puff pastry

5 tbsp. sugar

1 tsp. vanilla extract

1 large egg white

Directions:

1. Preheat air fryer to 350 degrees F. Line a baking sheet with parchment paper.
2. Combine the vanilla and sugar together.
3. Cut the puff pastry into two equal rectangles. Brush each with the egg white and sprinkle with sugar. Only use about half of the sugar. Place rectangles on top of each other. .
4. Cut into strips and sprinkle with remaining sugar. Bake for 15 minutes.
5. Cool and enjoy!

Chocolate Volcano Cake

(Total Time: 20 MIN | Serves: 8)

Ingredients:

2 cups semisweet chocolate chips, melted

2 tbsp. heavy cream

1 cup butter

4 eggs

4 egg yolks

½ cup sugar

2 tsp vanilla

½ cup flour

¼ cup cocoa powder

Directions:

1. Preheat fryer to 400 degrees. Spray a cake pan that fits into the fryer with nonstick spray

2. Mix the melted chocolate chips and heavy cream together until smooth. Set aside.

3. Combine all ingredients except for the flour and cocoa powder for about 5 minutes. Gradually add the flour and cocoa and mix until well combined

4. Place the chocolate and cream mixture into the center of the pan. Pour the batter over the top. Bake for 30 minutes.

5. Serve hot and enjoy!

Gran's Apple Cake

(Total Time: 35 MIN | Serves: 8)

Ingredients:

¼ cup butter

2 cups brown sugar

2 cups apples, chopped

2 cups dried cranberries, chopped

2 cups flour

2 large eggs

2 tsp baking soda

Directions:

1. Preheat fryer to 340 degrees F. Spray a cake pan that will fit into the air fryer with non-stick spray.

2. Mix the butter and the brown sugar until fluffy. Add the eggs and mix until combined.

3. Stir in remaining ingredients and pour the mixture into the prepared pan.

4. Bake for 35 minutes.

5. Cool completely, serve and enjoy!

Cherry Almond Cake

(Total Time: 35 MIN | Serves: 6)

Ingredients:

1 box white cake mix

½ cup vegetable oil

3 large eggs

½ cup water

1 can cherry pie filling

½ cup almonds, chopped

1 tsp. almond extract

Directions:

1. Preheat fryer to 350 degrees F.
2. Combine all ingredients except pie filling and mix well. Add the pie filling and carefully stir just until combined.
3. Pour into a cake pan sprayed with nonstick spray. Bake for 35 minutes.
4. Cool completely before serving.
5. Enjoy!

Lemon Berry Cake

(Total Time: 40 MIN | Serves: 6)

Ingredients:

½ cup vegetable oil

1 box lemon cake mix

3 eggs

½ cup water

1 cup fresh raspberries

1 cup fresh blueberries

½ cup powdered sugar

Directions:

1. Preheat air fryer to 325 degrees F.
2. Combine the oil, cake mix, eggs, and water. Mix until smooth. Gently fold in berries.
3. Pour the batter into a cake pan sprayed with nonstick spray. Bake for 25 minutes.
4. Cool completely and top with powdered sugar.
5. Serve and enjoy!

Lazy Dump Cake

(Total Time: 40 MIN | Serves: 6)

Ingredients:

2 (15oz) cans sliced peaches in
   heavy syrup

1 box vanilla cake mix

½ cup butter

1 tsp. ground cinnamon

Directions:

1. Preheat the air fryer to 350 degrees F.
2. Pour the peaches into a baking pan sprayed with nonstick spray.
3. Combine the butter, cinnamon, and cake mix just until crumbly. Pour over top of the peaches.
4. Bake for 30 minutes. Serve warm.
5. Enjoy!

Conclusion

Thank you again for purchasing this book!

I hope this Air Fryer Cookbook helps you understand the dynamics and principles of this revolutionary kitchen appliance, why you should use it and how it's going to change your outlook on food preparation and healthy living.

The next step is to get into the right frame of mind and decide that it's time to take charge of your eating habits by only putting the best organic and free range ingredients in your Air Fryer.

Even if you have never tried the Air Fryer before, I can promise you one thing, after the 30 days, you will be kicking yourself for having not discovered this sooner.

I hope it was able to inspire you to clean up your kitchen from all the useless appliances that clutter your countertop and start putting the Air Fryer to good use.

The Air Fryer is definitely a change in lifestyle that will make things much easier for you and your family. You'll discover increased energy, decreased hunger, a boosted metabolism and of course a LOT more free time!

I encourage you to share these recipes with family and friends, tell them about this book, and let them know that the Instant Pot can be the best investment that one can make.

Finally, if you feel that you have received any value from this book, then I'd like to ask if you would be kind enough to click on the link below and leave a review on Amazon to share your positive experience with other readers.

It'd be greatly appreciated!

Happy Air Frying!

Regards,

Luca Moretti

Printed in Great Britain
by Amazon